CONTENTS

Introduction

> *"One of the most striking
> differences between a cat
> and a lie is that a cat has
> only nine lives."*
> —MARK TWAIN,
> *Pudd'nhead Wilson*

Most people believe a lot of good, solid lies about the most basic and important aspects of owning and caring for a cat. I'm talking not only about neophytes but about people who have owned and loved cats for years and who consider themselves knowledgeable.

Misconceptions about neutering, declawing, feeding, breeding, and pedigrees abound. Lack of knowledge about behavior and health problems is woeful.

Often, the experts—vets, breeders, and pet shop owners—either will not or cannot be bothered to tell people the facts about their cats. Humane societies try to, but without much apparent success, because they tend to tell you what to do without explaining *why*.

In this book, I am setting forth not only what I believe to be the most accurate information and best methods, but why they are the best, and precisely how to apply this information to your cat.

The other day I told a woman that her female cats were suffering while they were in heat. She said, "My dear, I'm a biology teacher and I don't believe my cats suffer when in heat any more than *I* do when I get *my* period." This intelligent biology teacher didn't know that heat and menstruation are polar opposites, and that they involve entirely different kinds and degrees of suffering. If this woman believes such a myth, think of the rest of the public. I know—I've been talking to them for years.

I've never met a pet owner who wasn't grateful to be told the truth—not just the wherefores but the whys. People are invariably grateful, for instance, to learn what declawing actually entails instead of what vets allow them to believe. A genuinely viable alternative is music to their ears. I know— I'm speaking from firsthand experience.

For over ten years I have worked for Fabulous Felines, a Manhattan pet shop dealing exclusively with pedigreed cats, which has been in business for over twenty-five years, and I am now one of its owners. During this period of working and dealing with the public I have gotten a very clear idea of people's concerns about living with and training a cat. It is these concerns exclusively that I am dealing with in this book.

There is a well-known story of a schoolgirl who was assigned to write a report on a book about penguins. Her review—considered by many to be one of the great book reviews of all time—was: "This book told me more about penguins than I wished to know." I am not going to tell you more about cats than you wish to know, but I will tell you in detail what you *do* need to know.

Don't be put off by the fact that cat owners need a few simple instructions. Living with a good cat is the easiest thing in the world—and the rewards are tremendous. Spend an hour with this book and a small amount of training time, and you'll wonder how you ever managed to live without a cat!

1

CHOOSING
A CAT

KNOWING YOUR OWN MIND

When choosing a kitten, decide exactly what it is you want. Many people seem to be very muddled in their thinking when buying an animal, and the animal inevitably ends up paying for their mistakes.

For instance, some people I know got a Russian Blue from our store. The cat was very appealing and had a fabulous personality, but he was in no way close to being a prize-winner, which his owners understood and didn't mind at all. They loved him so much that they couldn't wait to get a second cat, and were all set to come back to us when they happened to go to a local cat show. There they saw an incredibly beautiful and flamboyant silver Persian and bought him immediately on the basis of his looks and his pedigree. It took the family barely two months to decide the Persian wasn't right for them. He was beautiful, but dumb, and not particularly affectionate. He just lay around all day looking gorgeous.

Many people would have loved that Persian. His aesthetic appeal and aloofness would have been just what they wanted. Simply watching him drape himself languidly on the chair that would show him to the best advantage would

3

have been a constant delight to the eyes. I only hope that he finally got a home with such people.

Of course, his original owners should have decided what they wanted in a pet before buying one. Certainly you can find both beauty and personality in one cat, but usually one quality will be more important to you than the other, so know yourself well enough to know which you value. Interestingly, if a certain type of beauty (really, they are all beautiful in different ways) is of primary importance, you will generally find the cat's personality attractive, and if his personality enchants you, he will take on a great physical appeal as well.

Let me give another example of muddled thinking. A man came into the shop and fell in love with an Abyssinian. He refused, however, to sign the alteration contract we require and finally left. He said that he had no wish to become a real breeder, or become part of the world of cat fancy. If he had bought an inexpensive cat he'd have been happy to alter it, but if he bought an expensive cat he felt he should get something in return in the way of championship kittens. It didn't seem right that he should pay all that money and not get some salable kittens.

I don't think the man was mercenary—just confused. He didn't want to be cheated. He knew perfectly well that stud fees and vet bills eat up most of the profits from breeding unless one has the facilities to breed on a large scale. He knew that the cat would have to go through many miserable periods of heat before and between being bred. He did not even want to breed as a hobby. He just had a vague, stubborn idea that you don't buy something expensive without getting a certain kind of use out of it.

I'm sure that he went someplace else and got exactly what he wanted. I'm also sure that he'll end up with neither a really good pet nor a financial bargain and that, as usual, it'll be the cat that pays. When the owner realizes the money he's spending in stud fees, vet bills for myriad kitten illnesses, and ads in newspapers trying to place the kittens (mostly in vain), he'll begin to resent the cat, particularly if she is becoming increasingly temperamental and driving him crazy with incessant calling. In the end, he'll get rid of her.

Again, it's a matter of the owner not finding out what he really wants. He has a general notion that things should turn out in a certain way. We are all unrealistic from time to time, and learn through our mistakes. That's how people *do* learn, through trial and error—finding out how the world really works, instead of how they thought it should work. In most cases it's only ourselves we harm during the painful process of learning, but in this case it's the animal. Those who cannot learn from the past are condemned to repeat it, George Santayana said. But many people never do learn, and it's the animals who are condemned. Each time such people get a new pet they wonder why it didn't turn out right. They decide that it's the cat's fault, and that if they try again with another, *next* time it'll work. For the owners, it hardly hurts at all—for the cat, it's a tragedy.

BRED CATS VS. DOMESTIC SHORTHAIRS

For many people, the fascination of the bred cat is the fascination of the world of cat fancy—the world of the professional and semiprofessional breeders and showers. It's a club, a hobby, a whole little world, and gives great pleasure and interest to many people. This is not my world, however, and I can't provide an exhaustive description of the various standards and the ideal appearance of each particular cat. I know what a good Abyssinian or Burmese looks like because I've seen so many, but I do not follow the ever-changing fads in shape of head, length of tail, and so on.*

To my mind, the advantage of the bred cats over the domestic shorthairs is that a certain type of breeder breeds for disposition more than for conformation to a set of physical standards. For my money, a good domestic shorthair is every bit as desirable as a good bred cat, but usually you can't tell before it's too late whether the cat will be sweet or aloof, hostile or friendly.

The breeders-for-disposition consistently produce cats with sweet, loving personalities, so if you want an affectionate pet, you're taking very little chance with a bred cat. Unfortunately, many of the big kitten-mill breeders concentrate so exclusively on physical characteristics that some highly bred cats are nervous, irritable, and unfriendly. This, to me, is a perversion of the whole idea of breeding.

BREEDING

The breeders-for-disposition truly love their animals and usually will not sell to most pet shops because most do not have a neuter/spay agreement (such as the humane organizations have), and because most make no effort to discourage declawing or to send the cat off with a good start—equipment, advice, etc. These breeders want their animals to find homes where they will be loved, treated well, and kept as good pets.

The cats sold by the breeders-for-disposition usually have pedigrees as good as the cats bred for cat-fancy and show. Since fads in physical conformations change like clothing fashions, a kitten with a non-prize-winning head

*See the Appendix for a general discussion of the various breeds.

by today's standard will often have parents and grandparents that won dozens of championships.

You will have to decide for yourself what you want. If you have your heart set on a real prize-winner, you should probably go to a breeder. If you want a good pet as well as a good pedigree, go to a pet shop that insists on neutering, and therefore has most likely spent years developing ties with the breeders who breed for disposition.

PEDIGREE AND REGISTRATION

While you are choosing your kitten, you are likely to hear people refer to a kitten's "papers." By this they mean a pedigree or registration, or both. A pedigree lists the names of the cat's parents, grandparents, great-grandparents, and so on, with the cattery of each, and any championships won. For instance, in "Purrfect's Nancy of Sinbad," "Purrfect" is the name of the cattery that bred the cat, "Nancy" is the cat's given name, and "Sinbad" is the name of the cattery of Nancy's present owner.

If a cattery owner wishes to register a cat, he sends in a form and a fee to one of the cat associations (American Cat Fancier's Association, Cat Fancier's Association, etc.). The association assigns a registration number to the particular cat or to the litter. This is necessary for record-keeping only if the cat is to be shown and bred. The associations provide no real supervision, however. In other words, no group or individual sends a staff of inspectors around to all the catteries to check which cat is actually being mated with which. Instead, the associations pretty much take the word of the individual cattery owner.

A pedigree can be verified only slightly more than a registration, because it's possible to look up old records and confirm that a certain cat actually *did* win a grand championship in a certain show. As far as I know, however, it's impossible to confirm that that grand-championship cat actually did father the kitten that the breeder said it did. Catteries are often out-of-the-way places and, as I've said, there's no real, meaningful supervision, so the buyer must rely on his estimate of the integrity of the breeder or of the shop selling the cat.

Many people believe that a cat's breeding can be determined only by its papers. On the contrary, this can be determined only by looking at the animal yourself or by having a trustworthy expert look at it.

I'm convinced that most breeders are as honest as possible about breeding and record-keeping. In my experience, however, most breeders, especially the good ones, hate paperwork and record-keeping. They are undeniably interested in the animals and their bloodlines, but would rather dig ditches than handle detailed paperwork. Instead, they rely on their professional judgment to determine whether a particular kitten is a good specimen, and more importantly, whether it has a bred-in good disposition. (I assume that the pedigrees of race horses, for example, are far more scrupulously maintained. Huge amounts of money ride on a particular horse, and stud fees are so staggering that it's necessary to have round-the-clock supervision by several people, keeping each other honest, to guarantee that a particular mare is impregnated by a particular stud.)

While some cats have the best papers in the world, one glance will tell you that they are poor examples of the breed—if they are of that breed at all. The margin for error is so great that your own eye, or your trust in someone with a more practiced eye, is the best criterion. So, forget about meaningless words on a piece of paper. Recording false information does not make the information true.

I often have a hard time explaining this to customers. Of

course, without any record-keeping, the cat fancy and the whole business of showing and judging would be impossible. But even at the shows, the judges look at the cat itself, not at pieces of paper.

When I tell a customer that a certain Siamese is not pedigreed, they think I mean it isn't a pure Siamese. Our store often deliberately chooses nonpedigreed Siamese because many people prefer round heads to long, thin ones, and also because our Siamese cats have been bred for marvelous dispositions. I always have to explain that the breeder didn't register and show these animals because they don't conform to present standards and could not win any prizes, although they are nonetheless pure Siamese.

We also carry two types of Russian Blues, one of which is unmistakably Russian Blue, while the other is indistinguishable from a blue domestic shorthair. I am fully aware that this second type is indeed a Russian Blue and fully registered and pedigreed, for whatever it's worth, but I also know that it wouldn't win any prizes, at least not at this writing. I always make this quite clear to the customer, because we sell both types for the same price since we feel they're equally valuable.

WHERE TO BUY A CAT

I have noticed, from time to time, ads in a major financial publication for large franchised chains of "department stores for pets." The parent company supplies the "merchandise" and advises the franchisee on how to turn a good profit. One of these businesses advertises that it has 160 outlets in regional malls. When such a company becomes this big—or is even one-tenth this size—the animals are purchased from big "kitten mills" and treated as "merchandise," with cost-accounting figuring out exactly how many kittens can be allowed to become sick and die while still showing a profit for the store.

People who work on a regular basis in a store that is not owner-operated usually have not been hired for their love of animals. In fact, they have probably come to resent the animals, since cleaning cages, changing kitty litter, and other such tasks are dirty work. The people actually in charge often have many stores, and are running the business from a separate office. They do not see the animals.

Can you imagine what you will probably get when you buy from one of these "outlets"? A kitten churned out for quantity rather than quality, with little concern by others for its disposition; a kitten which has been handled like merchandise from the time of its birth until the time it comes into your home. If a fine set of papers comes with the animal (see the section on pedigree), you will pay a staggering amount because there are so many middlemen and because good mall locations are very expensive.

This is exactly why breeders who care, and therefore have really good pets, will not sell to ordinary pet shops. So, beware if the shop's location is obviously expensive; beware if there is not a working, caring owner on the premises; and beware if the shop is one of several outlets in your town or city, and God knows how many all over the country. Of course you may get lucky—in fact many people do, or such places would go out of business—but you will be equally lucky, and maybe luckier, at your local pound.

If you acquire a kitten from some other source—a breeder, an ad in the paper, or a friend—subtly try to find out what the seller feels is important in an animal and make sure that you have decided what is important to you. Don't telegraph what it is you are interested in—ask what is particularly desirable about this particular litter and then *lis-*

ten. If the seller emphasizes blood lines and championships with little or no mention of temperament, be sure that disposition is of secondary importance to you as well.

DISPOSITION

When you choose a cat or kitten, there are a few superficial indications of disposition that you might bear in mind. The two most common and obvious indicators of a cat's disposition and state of mind at any given moment are the purr and the tail switch. Unlike dogs, cats signal momentary annoyance when they switch their tails. This is purely temporary and not in any way as serious as a puffed-up tail and an arched back. (I mean arched in the middle, not at the base of the tail. All cats, even small kittens, will instinctively raise their hind quarters toward your hand when stroked.) A tail switch merely means "you just took my favorite chair away" or "I don't feel like being held at just this moment, if you don't mind," and can be changed into "I guess that feels pretty good after all" in half a second.

A purr, on the other hand, indicates that the cat is happy and pleased with whatever is going on at the moment. Some cats purr very loudly and can be heard all the way into the next room. Others purr almost inaudibly, and the only way to detect it is by putting your finger on the cat's throat. If you can feel a vibration almost like a running motor, the cat is purring. Often a cat's whole body vibrates, but unless you feel the cat's throat you may not know if the cat is purring or trembling.

If a kitten purrs the minute you pick him up, you can be pretty sure that he is people-oriented and is likely to be very friendly and loving. The absence of a purr, however, does not necessarily imply aloofness. Some cats never, or very rarely, purr. My cat Barny, for instance, purrs only when he is planning to nurse on my blouse or nightgown. He reserves his purr strictly for the anticipation of regressing to kittenhood and doing now what was then denied him (he was the runt of the litter and always pushed aside at feeding time). Barny is, however, at all times a true gentleman and has natural good manners. If he wants to get under the covers, he taps my hand or my face with a velvet paw until I make an opening for him—it's like a polite knock on the door. He also does this to get my attention at other times—a truly delicate way to make a request.

When picking a kitten, look first for a purr. If it is absent, look for other signs of either gentleness or hostility, but don't mistake temporary fear for hostility. Ask the owner or manager about the disposition of the animal. An honest shop owner who loves the animals and wants the best for them will give you a truthful evaluation of the cat's personality. He knows that different people have different tastes, and that it's to his own as well as to the cat's advantage to tell the truth.

MALE VS. FEMALE

Half the customers who come into our store are convinced that males are more affectionate than females. Guess what? The other half are convinced that females are more affectionate than males.

It seems to me that the differences in temperament, affection, and tractability have to do with breeding for disposition and individual characteristics rather than gender. Those convinced that one sex is more loving than the other have probably met nicer males than females, or vice versa. Similarly, neither sex has specific talents, such as being a good mouser or having the ability to fetch like dogs.

There are, of course, physical differences between the sexes: within a given litter, males tend to be slightly bigger and females slightly hardier, especially in kittenhood. If unaltered, females are more prone to ovarian and breast tumors, false pregnancies, etc. Males, altered and unaltered, are more prone to urinary calculus (discussed in chapter 3).

It is more expensive to alter a female than a male, but there are now many low-cost neuter/spay clinics, so that the financial difference is not great. Similarly, since the operation on the female is more complicated, there is slightly more risk, but since the main risk in routine operations involves anesthesia, which both operations require, the difference remains negligible.

If you already have a cat and plan to get a second, I don't think it much matters whether the second is of the same sex, assuming, of course, that both cats are or will be altered. Many people feel that cats of opposite sexes get along better, but my two altered males adore each other, in spite of the fact that the age difference between them (a much more significant factor) is seven years.

My oldest cat, Schatzie, a female, has never liked any other cat, or any person, other than me, and sometimes she has her doubts about me—in fact, often! I got her by chance—before I knew anything about cats—and though she will always have a good home with me, I will never again adopt such a very young kitten without knowing what kind of personality it will be likely to develop. Schatzie hates my two males, who have always tried their best to be friendly.

When Barny, my older male, was seven, I brought home Waddy, to whom Barny was perfectly polite, but who drove Barny crazy wanting to play and pounce all the time. He'd play for a while, then start to grumble, and would finally give Waddy a whack. Waddy would cry for five minutes, and then come back for more. He didn't mind being whacked as long as he could be close to Barny.

Now that Waddy is two years old and no longer a kitten, the two are totally contented with each other, and sleep and play for the same amount of time, though Barny might prefer a little less play and a little more sleep.

CAT AND MOUSE

Some people get cats in order to get rid of mice. As far as I know, there is no way to tell ahead of time whether a cat or kitten is going to be good at catching mice. One theory is that kittens learn from their mothers, and therefore, if you want a good mouser you'd better get a cat brought up in a farmer's barn by its mother. From my own observation, this doesn't seem to be true. I've seen cats born in catteries where there were no mice, or taken away from their mothers before they could learn mouse-catching, who were absolutely superb mousers, and I've seen street cats who were utterly indifferent.

The size and disposition seem to make no difference either. A fluffy, delicate-boned, purry little creampuff with a bow in her hair that has been overfed by a doting owner all her life may decimate an entire mouse population with unbelievable efficiency—one whack per mouse and you have as many corpses lying around as in the last act of *Hamlet*! A big, tough street cat, on the other hand, may just sit and look at a mouse with pleasant interest and curiosity without having the slightest desire to kill it.

The mere presence of a cat, however, should substantially lower your mouse population. Most mice will seek other lodgings if there's a cat in the house, even if he's not a good mouser.

But don't get a cat only for the sake of getting rid of

mice. If you think of your cat as nothing but an animated exterminator, you will resent even the little time and trouble your cat will require, and the services of a reliable exterminating firm will be less difficult and less costly in the end. If you really do want a cat and feel it would be a nice bonus if the mice went away, you'll probably be lucky—but pick the cat for his own sake, not solely for the purpose of catching mice. Mouse-catching seems to be a game to cats, and, as I will explain later, each cat makes up his own games. For one cat, efficient extermination is fascinating, while another would rather play fetch with a piece of cellophane.

HOW OLD SHOULD YOUR NEW PET BE?

You are better off buying a kitten when it's at least ten weeks old. I know, you want a little tiny kitty six weeks old or less—but you and the kitten are better off if you wait. After all, you're going to live with this cat for approximately seventeen years, so it's silly to fool around with his personality by taking him away from his mother too soon for the sake of a few extra weeks of kittenhood. Also, if you're buying from a pet shop, it's better to give the kitten a little time in a cage. Surprisingly, they often make better pets—more used to depending on and relating exclusively to humans—if they've had some time in a cage.

Some of the best buys in the pet world are the slightly older animals—those unsold until they are five, six, or even seven months old. Don't assume that because a cat didn't get sold quickly there must be something wrong with him. Often, many kittens of the same breed come in to a store at one time, and one may be left by pure happenstance. Or a kitten may have had a minor ailment, such as a cold or a bad eye, and needed time to recover before becoming salable. Ask the owner or manager, and if the answer is reasonable, rely on your own feelings. If you feel warmth toward the cat, go ahead and get it, and don't worry.

Most pet shops lower the price as the kittens get older because people want them as young as possible and because the tiny ones are so cute. If you're willing to sacrifice the teeny-tiny phase, you'll not only get a bargain financially, but you'll often get a better cat. His disposition has formed by this time, so when you hold him you know he will continue to respond to you as he does now. Also, he's accustomed to thinking of human beings as the source of all good things and will readily adore you and your home.

Older kittens may require a little more time to adjust, not to you but to the open space of your home. Because they've spent much of their lives in cages, larger spaces confuse them and they tend to stay under the sofa for a longer period—perhaps a week instead of a day. This timidity soon passes, however, and with a little patience and understanding you'll end up with a fabulous cat.

OLDER CATS

One of the nicest things you can do in this world is to adopt an older cat who would otherwise have trouble finding a home. These animals crave and appreciate love and affection. If you know the fundamentals of training, you will end up with a wonderful pet and the satisfaction of having done a good deed. In fact, your only disadvantage might be foregoing the young-kitten stage—a stage that many people find quite trying.

Often people who would really rather have a slightly older, less rambunctious, and more civilized cat fear that the cat's personality is already formed and that he will never be really "theirs" in the sense that he would have been had they raised him. These fears are unfounded. Whether the cat has been out on the streets fighting for his life or in a cage being taken care of but deprived of freedom and close personal attention, he will let you know right away if he wants a home and loves people. Unlike a kitten, whose personality you have no way of predicting (unless he has been bred for disposition), the mature cat who indicates a desire to love and be loved is a sure bet to become yours with an unsurpassable gratitude and desire to please.

An exception might be a cat over ten years old. If he's been in a cage or somebody's beloved pet for that long, he will probably (though not always) be a little too old to adjust to a new situation. You'll be able to judge by his reaction to you.

If a cat has been on the streets, he won't be that old. If, by some miracle, he's still alive on the streets at age ten, he's such an old pro that he'll survive. Give another cat a chance.

If you do adopt a young adult, you should take him to a vet and give him a distemper shot if he hasn't had one within a year. If you have no way of knowing, a second shot won't hurt him, whereas the lack of one could easily kill him.

A cat that's been on the streets will probably also have minor and relatively unimportant ailments—fleas, mites, skin problems, worms—all of which a vet should attend to, and none of which should be costly or troublesome (see the chapter on minor ailments).

A cat that's been in a cage may be afraid of space for a

while—all that vastness is confusing—but this fear will
gradually vanish. He will also have already learned to de-
pend on people for his every need. If he's been on the
street, the cat may be wary at first—for good reason. But
once he realizes that you are a friend—which often takes
the cat only a few hours to recognize—he'll respond and
be almost pathetically grateful.

WILD CATS

Many people ask me if I can help them find an ocelot, a
puma, or even a leopard. Fortunately, these and other wild
animals are illegal in New York, and should be in the entire
country.

Almost all wild animals that people can buy have been
acquired by sending someone into the jungle to shoot the
mother and grab the babies, most of whom do not then
survive. That's why they're so expensive. If you do manage to get one and to keep it healthy, you yourself will be
forced, even with the best intentions, to practice cruelty.

It's not natural for wild beasts who long for freedom to
be kept in apartments and walked on leashes. I know that
they can be extremely affectionate and receptive to training, but a side of their nature can never be satisfied by
human companionship. Most people eventually have them
declawed, even detoothed, and finally donate them to a
zoo. Of course, you're certain that you'd never do that.
But ask yourself how you'd react the first time you're
really scared—when your very strong and large pet re-
verts, even momentarily, to this other nature. Won't you be
frightened of him ever after? And won't that lead to loving
him less, keeping him penned up, mutilating his body?

If it doesn't bother you, if you feel that the cat has

already been captured and the mother shot, so you're not doing anything that hasn't already been done anyway, remind yourself that if people didn't buy these cats, the whole business would collapse very quickly.

2

PREPARING AND CARING FOR YOUR NEW CAT

NAMING THE CAT

Like any other new member of your household, your new kitten needs a name right away. Some people find it very difficult to think up names for their cats. They want the name to be perfect: terribly original, not too cute, not too human, ideally suited to the particular cat's nature. A certain type of person often will not name the animal at all, and end up calling his pet "You" or "Cat" because he worries that he will look too sentimental in giving the cat a name, or that the name won't be perfect. Other people with this problem will literally wait months before naming the cat anything at all, and then still not be happy with the name.

Give your cat a name immediately—preferably on the first day. The bond between you and your cat will be much stronger if he has a real name that is his and only his from the beginning. He will be more secure, responsive, and better adjusted if he is always called by the same name; and he will acquire a real, separate identity in your mind, and therefore in his, if he has a "title" to be identified by.

You can forget about originality. Almost anything you can think of has already been used, and so what? In fact, if

23

it's too original—given for no reason other than original-ity—it will lessen, not reinforce, the bond between the two of you. The cat will seem more like a walking joke than like a living, sentient creature. In other words, name him "Beowulf," for instance, only if you really are an Old English scholar and the name really has a personal and pleasant significance for you.

I would strongly suggest avoiding all unpleasant names. During World War II people sometimes called their pets "Adolf" or "Tojo" in a misguided attempt at cleverness. I have seen cats whose owners dearly love them but who nevertheless have names like "Stupid" or "Ugly." You should avoid such names because even though you and your cat understand that he is delightful and that you love him, other people may not get the point and will subcon-sciously feel contempt for or hostility toward an animal called something unattractive. I can't help feeling that you, too, will acquire a callous attitude toward your cat if you constantly call him "Stupid," and that you will transmit this attitude to him.

These cautions aside, anything that appeals to you is fine, as long as you give it to him right away without wor-rying too much. People's names, place names, anything will do. As soon as it's really his, it will become him and not simply a name, and you'll wonder why you worried about it in the first place.

Occasionally, the cat himself will give you a clue. My cat Waddy was originally called Waddo (short for Wad-dington, from a personal experience of mine). Anyway, he just wouldn't respond to Waddo, although he'd certainly had plenty of time to learn his name properly and would respond when I called the other cats. I finally realized that both my other cats had names ending in "y," and when I called him "Waddy" he responded immediately. He figured that all proper cats had names ending in "y" and he wanted one too, just like the other guys.

A well-loved cat, like a well-loved child, will usually have lots of pet names. At various times I call Waddy "Waddo," "Waddington," "Wadsville," "Waddle," "The Wad," and "Silliness."

Almost every affectionate cat will come when he hears his name called. He won't come in the same manner as a dog. He will saunter out a few minutes after being called as if he just happened to feel like it anyway, but he will come —not out of obedience but because he really *does* happen to feel like it when his favorite person calls. Yes, he takes time to think it over. Yes, he'll postpone it if he's stalking a fascinating fly or taking a thorough bath. And yes, sometimes he'll decide he doesn't feel like it at all. But when he does come, which is most of the time, it's a real compliment.

Bringing Home Your New Kitten

Bring your new kitten home in a carrier. If he's not in a carrier, he could easily jump out of your arms. Remember, he's already nervous and doesn't know you—let one car backfire and he'll jump out of your arms and run, probably never to be found again. Your pet shop will usually supply a temporary carrier free of charge rather than let you take this risk. If your pet shop doesn't supply one, either buy one, since you'll need it later anyway, or construct a temporary one from a cardboard box from the grocery store— but make sure it's securely fastened with tape.

The best carriers are enclosed rather than transparent on the top. The cat will probably never like his carrier anyway, but if he has to be in one, he'll prefer a secure, enclosed, womblike atmosphere. To have to look out at a strange jumble of scary new things makes the experience worse from his point of view, literally and figuratively.

If you're fairly sure that he'll only be in his carrier for short periods—a ten-minute trip to the vet now and then —a small one will do and will be much easier for you. If he's going to be in it for hours, of course the carrier must be bigger.

A good idea is a soft carrier shaped like a flight bag or an old-fashioned carpet bag. Because they are pliant, they are easier to carry and can rest on the seat or the floor on long car trips. The cat can then crawl in at will when he wants a secure, protected feeling. You won't usually find these sold as cat carriers per se, so you may find it necessary to poke a few holes in them for air.

Once you have safely brought your kitten home, you should show him his box before doing anything else. Make sure to have this ready if your pet shop does not automatically provide one. Plump him right into the middle of the litter. He will get out immediately and start exploring, or he may possibly hide at first, but in any case, when he needs his box, he'll think, "Where's that great place where I can cover it up?" and he'll go right to it. Burying his trail is a deep instinct in the cat, which explains why it's no trouble to train a cat to his box. This also explains why cats become neurotic in metal mesh-bottomed cages in which the excrement falls through the holes—they can't cover it up to their satisfaction and they worry. The same holds true for torn-up newspaper.

Every instinct tells the cat, unlike a dog, to go to the box. As long as it's kept reasonably clean, he will always use it. I therefore don't recommend kits that train a cat to the toilet; they may work temporarily, but you're interfering with a basic instinct, and a good one from your point of view. Don't tamper with it.

Any good clay litter will do. You'll find that the brands in the supermarket will vary. One brand will be overly dusty and smelly for a few months, and another a few months later. You'll just have to play this by ear.

Green chlorophyll litter is often unappealing to cats and many will become untrained because of it. Also avoid perfumed litter—cats don't like it. Stick to the regular tan colored clay litter. You can mix some baking soda in the litter if you like—many people swear by it—but I find it easy enough to keep the box clean and odor-free without it. For the feces, get a large spoon with a slotted bowl and scoop whenever necessary. For the rest, your nose will tell you when to change the litter. You can use either a little litter and change it every day, or a lot and change it every few days. Clumps of saturated litter can be lifted out separately, leaving the rest until the whole thing is ready to be changed.

After you acquaint your cat with the litter box, put up the exercise post and show it to him. In a few days, if necessary, you will start training him to it (see the section on the exercise post).

After that, take your lead from the kitten. Some kittens will start to play immediately, while some will be nervous and hide. If yours seems shy and retiring for the first few days, or even for a week or ten days, do not assume he will always be a timorous beast. Some of the most loving and affectionate cats have taken a long period of adjustment before they finally let their personalities show. Don't try to grab your cat or haul him out from under the bed or force his affection. He will come out eventually and will suddenly want to come to you. You can speak lovingly to him, but don't grab; play hard to get. When you least expect it— plump! He'll be on your lap asking to be stroked and fondled. At this point you should try to spend as much time

Diagram 1

as possible with him for a few days. Once you've estab-
lished a real bond with him by giving him "prime time" in
the beginning, you've got a wonderful pet for life.

Cats are very physical and respond to touch and sound.
The best way to hold a nervous new cat or kitten is to
support his bottom and hold him in such a way that all four
paws are against your body, as shown in diagram 1. After
he's used to you, and particularly to so much space, and
has lost his nervousness, you can hold him almost any way
you like and he'll be delighted. But if he's in any way
nervous or scared, he'll feel more secure held safely
against your body without his legs dangling in the air.

Many people believe that because the mother cat carries
her kittens around by the scruff of the neck, that's the best
way to do it. It's fine for very young kittens, but it's damaging to an older, heavier cat. Always support his body,
even if you're gripping the back of his neck in order to

control him (which is usually unnecessary).

Fondle your cat, feel all over his body and see what type of touch pleases him and where he wants to be rubbed. You'll love the reaction you get. Talk to him softly and caressingly in a special tone of voice reserved just for him. In this way, you are imprinting him and he'll always love you.

Sooner or later, your cat will explore your apartment or house thoroughly, and I mean thoroughly—including insides of closets, cabinets, and any drawers left open. Cats love to get into small, enclosed spaces, and their ingenuity is amazing. Never shut doors and drawers without making sure that your cat's not in there. Always be careful, also, about slamming doors, especially the refrigerator door, when your cat might have tuck his curious little head in or out for a quick peek. Cats can also get all the way into the refrigerator with disastrous results if you're not on the lookout.

Remember not to roughhouse with the kitten. This is a real temptation, because he will love it and so will you and especially children. Kittens that play rough are adorable, but they're not so adorable once they become cats. If you've gotten a kitten into the habit of frenzied, rough play, it's going to be very hard to get him to unlearn this when he's big enough so that his claws and teeth can really hurt; then, "play" is suddenly a real nuisance. Of *course* you should play with him—the more often the better—but stop immediately when he loses control in the excitement of the game. Train him to be gentle with you always and to expect gentleness from you.

Finally, if you have small, valuable objects sitting around, remove them at first. Once he's out of the clumsy phase, and especially after he is thoroughly familiar with every inch of your house and every small object in it, you

really won't have to worry, for cats are astonishingly grace-
ful and can easily tiptoe around delicate things without
breaking them.

However, do not leave flat, small, light objects, such as
a wristwatch or a ring, on an inviting surface. At any age,
your cat will play with something like this, deliberately
pushing it off with tiny playful shoves. Don't discipline
him for this—it's his nature. In fact, give him something
you don't care about to play with, as well as a few toys of
his very own.

If you're a smoker, a rolled-up cigarette pack makes a
wonderful toy. It's light and crunchy-sounding and your cat
will bat it around for hours. Many cats will even fetch like
dogs, which always bowls over cat owners, but this is in
fact quite common. A wine-bottle cork is also a good toy,
though not as crunchy. It's light and can't hurt the cat. A
rabbit's foot (not the kind with a metal top—just a plain,
ordinary rabbit's foot) is also a favorite. It still has a slight
animal smell (discernible to him, not to you) and he'll stalk
his prey for hours. Sometimes cats eat these with no apparent ill consequences, but usually they just hide the toys and
bring them out again months later. Noisier toys like ping-
pong balls are also fun for the cat, but since your cat will
often hide these along with the rest of his toys, you won't
be able to put them away at night and he may wake you at
dawn by batting them around.

When you're preparing for your new cat's arrival, don't
waste money on a cat bed. He'll much prefer to sleep with
you or on your best chair, and there's no reason that he
shouldn't. He will not keep you awake when he's under the
covers with you, and you won't squash him even if you
roll over in your sleep. I don't know how cats avoid this,
but they always do. They especially like to sleep with two
people in the same bed, one paw on each.

As for the furniture, there's no reason why he shouldn't

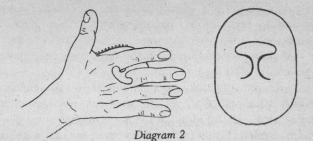

Diagram 2

lie on it as long as he doesn't scratch (which he won't if properly trained—see the exercise post section in this chapter). Cats keep themselves very clean and will not in any way hurt or dirty your furniture. It's the nature of a cat to get up on furniture, not stay down on the floor. Don't expect to train him as you would a dog. He's a different kind of beast with different needs, and expecting him to lie on the floor like a dog is not only unnecessary but ignores his instincts.

However, your cat is bound to shed. Let's face it, all animals with hair shed. You and I shed—at least I do—so if someone tells you that a certain type of cat won't shed, don't believe him. Long-haired cats don't shed more than short-haired ones, it's just that what they shed is longer. Cats like the Rex, who have much less hair, don't shed quite as much, but it's harder to clean up their shed hair because of its fine, downy quality. The right diet and brushing the cat once a day will help. Those little plastic brushes sold in men's barber shops are ideal (diagram 2), but you may use anything that does the job—you'll be able to tell once you start brushing. Don't brush for too long or too hard, or you'll hurt his skin and he won't like it. Otherwise, he'll adore being brushed.

The best tool I've found for taking cat hair off the furniture is something called a "magik brush," which can usually be found at ten-cent stores. It's made of stiff material with all the pile or nap going one way, and it works beautifully (diagram 3). You might also wish to purchase "tack cloth" from your hardware store. This cloth is sticky —wonderful for dusting and many other household chores as well as for taking up cat hair.

If you're really lucky, your cat will let you vacuum him, which is the best of all possible solutions, but don't count on it! Most cats are afraid of the noise, though some don't seem to mind. I didn't think of this until my cats were too old, but if you start yours on it as a kitten you may get him to like it.

Of course, you'll have a nail clipper and clip his nails (again, see the section on the exercise post).

If your cat must be on a leash occasionally for some reason, get a collar rather than a harness. In the first place, cats always seem able to get out of harnesses, no matter how secure they look, and in the second place, most harnesses I've seen seem to be made for dogs—harnesses hit the cat in the wrong places, and interfere with the movement of his legs. The cat can't be left alone on a collar and leash because he could hang himself, but he couldn't be left alone on a harness either.

Finally, I can't emphasize enough that you must give a new kitten a chance—at least two weeks—before you make any big decisions. If in his nervousness he hides, makes mistakes on your rug, or seems terrified of you, bear in mind that those are temporary problems. Whatever real or permanent problems you might have (let's hope there won't be any) will be entirely different from those of the first two weeks. Try to remember why you wanted a kitten, and keep those reasons firmly in mind during this initial phase.

Or perhaps you have another cat who, instead of attacking the kitten as you expected, seems afraid of him, and this makes you feel guilty. What have you done to your

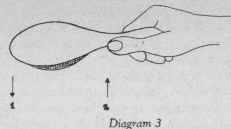

1   2

Diagram 3

wonderful baby who is now reluctant to sit in your lap because the kitten is stealing his thunder? Relax. The kitten, being young and recently released from a cage, has so much energy that he is driving the older cat crazy. The older cat is not so much fearful as he is sick of being pestered. As soon as the young one settles down, the real relationship between them will develop. They will get to like each other and curl up in each other's arms and groom each other. Chances are this will happen, although you don't believe it at first. By the time your new kitten grows up, whichever cat winds up as "top cat" won't matter much since both of them will be happy with the new arrangement. With luck, neither will be top cat—they'll be separate but equal. (See the section about introducing a new cat into a one-cat household.)

NEUTERING

Much of the cruelty in this world is caused by simple greed, plus a large dose of laziness, and nowhere is this better exemplified than in the attitude of most pet-shop personnel and breeders toward neutering.

I have been dealing with the public for over seven years, and I have almost never come across a customer who wasn't anxious to treat his cat in the best and kindest way. Most new pet owners, however, have a vague idea that neutering is cruel—they wouldn't want to be neutered themselves, so why do it to a beloved pet? The fact is that unless an animal is bred properly by a professional, he suffers intensely if not altered.

An unaltered male cat needs to mate all the time. Breeding him every now and then drives him crazy. He wants to breed and breed and breed, sometimes several times per hour. You can let him do this only if you have a cattery with seven or eight females for every male. The female breeds only when she is in heat. Once she becomes pregnant, which happens quickly, she is out of commission as far as breeding is concerned—she cannot and will not mate. It takes approximately two months until the kittens are born, and another two months more until they are weaned. After that, she should go through several heats before being bred again so that her system is not overly taxed. This works out to about two breedings per year for any one given female. What does the male cat do during the rest of the time? Goes crazy, that's what!

The same holds true for a female who is unaltered and allowed to have a litter once in a while so the kiddies can witness the miracle of birth. If unmated, she will go into heat more and more often as she grows older, and for greater and greater periods of time. These intervals vary widely from cat to cat. During these periods of heat, she will yell and roll around, obviously driven to desperation by a force that she can't control.

Unaltered, the male must be at it all the time and so must the female—mating, being pregnant, nursing, mating, being pregnant, and nursing. No one can cope with this endless cycle except a professional breeder with a cattery, many females for each male, and a large setup for the breeding and rearing of kittens. If you can't provide this, the only humane alternative is to have the cat altered.

An unaltered animal past the age of eight months, male

or female, lives in a state of sexual tension that is highly stressful and can manifest itself in many ways. Because of the constant tension, females often get ovarian cysts, false pregnancies, even cancer. Both males and females often develop peculiar behavior patterns, such as eating nonfood items (wood, glue, etc.), acting strangely, and exhibiting generally neurotic behavior directly caused by stress. Perhaps you have an unaltered cat that doesn't seem bothered in the least—wait and see. You can't always detect the stress since the cat can't talk, but it's there, and may sooner or later show up in a very painful way, even, perhaps, in the form of premature death.

If you want your female to have just one litter of kittens and then alter her, ask yourself why—could it be for your own amusement? It's not better for her health to have at least one litter. On the contrary, she'll be more susceptible to physical troubles. All humane societies now insist on alteration as a condition of adoption and they would not do this if it were bad for the female cat. In fact, female cats who are not spayed run a higher risk of severe uterine infection and mammary tumors.

The current huge overpopulation of animals represents a serious problem. Humane societies destroy fourteen million animals each year, more than half of them cats. Millions more die agonizing deaths on the streets, the victims of accidents, starvation, or brutality. There are simply not enough homes for all the homeless animals.

If you have at least four friends who would love to have a kitten, *your* kittens would certainly find homes. I know from experience that timing is everything when acquiring animals. A friend who sincerely wanted a kitten six months ago is now in a different phase and not interested. However, having committed himself, he might take it anyway. Guess what happens? An animal that is not really wanted is an animal with a good chance of being neglected and oth-

erwise mistreated. You've read what people do to unwanted children. Think what people, even nice people, do
to unwanted pets.

If my arguments about kindness to animals haven't convinced you, think about kindess to yourself. An unaltered
male will spray and the smell is dreadful. He will urinate
all over your household and his urine will contain the smell
of the male hormone, which may be delightful to female
cats, but believe me, it won't be delightful to you.

By spraying, a cat is marking off sexual territory—a
deep instinct in male cats and, incidentally, dogs. Have you
noticed that when you take a female dog for a walk she will
immediately squat and urinate, but a male dog will do a
little here and a little there, all over the neighborhood? He
is telling all the other dogs that this is his territory and that
all females in this area belong to him.

You may not mind this with a dog because he sprays
outside, but do you want a male cat to spray inside your
house? If not, you'll have to pen him up, which is cruel,
and which in any case prevents him from being a good
companion. Many people, not understanding the reason for
this sudden spraying, simply abandon the cat to die in the
street, not because they are cruel but because the people
who should have forewarned them—the original sellers—
couldn't be bothered or may not have wanted to miss a
sale!

When your female is in heat, she doesn't spray, but she
calls and rolls around, never giving you any peace, and
eventually she becomes spiteful. So does the male, if kept
too long in an unnatural state of semicelibacy. If altered,
however, cats of both sexes will retain the sweet kitten
disposition forever.

Unless for some specific reason your vet advises otherwise, males should be altered at seven months of age and
females at eight. This allows their bodies to attain maturity

but is early enough to ward off spraying in the male or repeated heats in the female. Sometimes a vet will advise waiting longer in the case of a very small cat or one with a delicate system. Sometimes a female will start heats prematurely, at four or five months. In this case, discuss the timing with your vet.

Some vets recommend using torn-up newspaper instead of litter in the box for a week after neutering a male cat. I think this is unnecessary as well as confusing and upsetting to the cat, and bothersome to the owner. I've always used litter and have never had bad results. Why overprotect an animal against all possible eventualities and upset the cat owner? And who's to say that newsprint is better than litter if it should happen to get into the cat's very tiny incision?

There are a few methods for spaying a female. Almost every vet in New York makes a very long incision in the middle of the cat's stomach. With this type of incision, the healing process is much longer than with two short incisions. There is a danger that the wound would open up if the cat weren't kept confined, thus necessitating five to seven (or more) days of expensive boarding with the vet, or a second, expensive trip to have the stitches removed, or both. Since approximately four inches of stomach muscle have been cut, it is harder for the cat to regain muscle tone after this type of operation, and the stomach may sag permanently.

The method I prefer involves making a very small incision, about the diameter of a quarter, or if the vet is very able, the diameter of a dime, and making this incision on the side. This requires a little more skill and care from the vet and therefore, I suppose, entails a bit more risk, but the advantages so outweigh the liabilities that, in my opinion, there's no comparison. The cat may leave the hospital as soon as the anesthetic has worn off, and there's no danger of stitches breaking open if she jumps around and plays.

Also, her stomach muscles have not been severed, since the incision was made on the side. Finally, the vets who perform this type of spay use a thread that dissolves naturally in time, so you need not take your cat back to the vet to have stitches removed.

DECLAWING

Declawing is painful and don't let anyone tell you that it isn't. I've seen older cats cry from pain for days after having been declawed, and I've had countless cat owners tell me that if they'd known what they were putting the cat through, they wouldn't have done it.

I certainly agree that you can't let your furniture be ruined, but I don't see why so few experts (vets and pet-shop owners) don't even suggest alternatives. It's not enough merely to buy an expensive exercise post; you have to know how to train the cat to use it. Resort to declawing only if all else fails.

Many people believe that declawing removes only the nails. On the contrary, the whole knuckle is removed. The cat has to relearn how to walk in a different, less natural, and less agile way. Declawing is a serious mutilation, not just a thorough manicure.

A second gruesome fact about declawing—the cats, of course, can't tell you and the experts simply won't—is that the nails may grow back inside the paw. They grow back gnarled, crooked, and invisible to you, but the cat's paws are then permanently sore. This is one reason that declawed cats often become mean or depressed—they are in constant pain. If you do have declawed cats, I suggest that their paws be X-rayed every few years to check for these mutant claws. Pressing the paw to see if the pressure seems to hurt won't do. The animal will be so accustomed to sore paws that an extra press or two won't elicit any unusual response. This doesn't happen often, but it's common enough so that you should bear this risk in mind when considering declawing.

Some people who own declawed animals say that their pets don't seem to mind. I hope they're right. One common fallacy, however, is that the cat still thinks he has nails because he makes clawing motions on the furniture. From this, people conclude that if the cat thinks he has nails he's just as well off as if he did have nails.

When declawed cats make clawing motions on the furniture, they are trying, in vain, to perform a basic and necessary cat exercise. This explains why I used the term "exercise post" instead of "scratching post." If the cat can't grip the post (or the furniture), he can't do a particular kind of back-stretching and pulling exercise that he obviously feels a deep need to perform. *This* is the reason that declawed cats always try to scratch. They know perfectly well that they are declawed, but feel driven to try again and again to get a grip (impossible without claws) in something so as to get the proper pull and stretch for their backs.

Finally, a declawed cat can't defend itself properly if threatened. Many cats manage amazingly well, even climbing trees, if only the front claws have been removed, but there is a psychological aspect to this issue. Even though cats may do very well at self-defense, they feel at a great disadvantage, and tend to put on a much bigger show of hostility and toughness in order to compensate for what they feel to be an inability to defend themselves. In some cases, their dispositions become permanently soured.

Let me reiterate that you should declaw a cat only if you cannot train him. A customer of mine told me that her Burmese had gone into a depression. After questioning her, I found the cat had just been declawed. I asked if she had been unable to train him and learned that he'd been per-

fectly trained, never scratched the furniture, never un-
sheathed his nails (there were children in the house), and
was very careful to be the perfect cat (a Burmese characteristic). I then asked why she'd had him declawed. She
said that her vet had suggested it, telling her that it was the
usual thing to do, without giving any other explanation.

Now, this vet clearly wanted to make another few dollars. He probably didn't particularly like cats (he was pri-
marily a cattle and horse vet), and my customer hadn't
bothered to ask if declawing was desirable or necessary. If
your vet suggests declawing without being asked, or
doesn't offer alternatives once asked, or suggests declawing all four feet instead of just the front feet (utterly unnecessary), get rid of him—he shouldn't be in the business.

I told the customer that her cat was depressed because
he missed his claws, particularly since he had done nothing
to deserve declawing. I advised her to give him lots of
extra love and affection to help him get over the depression. That's the best and only thing you can do once the
damage has been done, except for periodic re-examination
of the paws to make sure that they have not become sore
from unnoticed bone chips, regrowth of nails inside the
paw, etc.

A recently published translation of a German book says
that declawing is punishable under German animal protective law, and concludes, "A cat without its natural weapons
is like every other creature enslaved by man—it is no
longer itself!"*

---

*Dagmar Thies, *Cat care*, translated by Thomas Madero (Neptune City, NJ, TFH
Publications, 1980), pp. 55-56.

EXERCISE POST

Once your new kitten or cat has become accustomed to the house and has fallen madly in love with you, always wanting to be in the room with you, in your bed, and on your lap, you can start training him to use the exercise post. By this time, you'll have had opportunities to see if he is using it without training (many of them do), in which case you have no problem. Praise him extravagantly when he uses it and you'll have trained him effortlessly!

If, however, he's getting interested in your rugs and upholstery instead of or in addition to the post, and if telling him "NO" and placing his paws on the post doesn't work, try the following method of using the post.

Getting the Right Post

First, find an exercise post made of some material other than upholstery or rug material. This prevents the cat from confusing the type of upholstery material he *is* allowed to scratch with the type he isn't. Cork is very good (unless you have cork walls) and very satisfactory to the cat—he can get his nails into it and really stretch. If you can't find cork, try a post made of corrugated paper, and of a consistency so that the cat can get a grip on it. Perhaps some type of wicker or rattan would do, or material from a doormat, or a rope rug, or the reverse side of a piece of carpeting. Make sure it's one that you can attach to the wall at whatever height is right for the cat, raising it as he grows bigger. Most cats like to get up on their hind legs and scratch at a 45-degree angle, so let the size of the cat determine the height of the post (diagram 4).

The post must be securely anchored, which is why I don't like the kind on stands. Unless the post is terribly heavy or nailed to the floor, the cat can pull it down on himself. If this happens even once, he'll be afraid and won't use it again.

If you have a very big wicker basket that you don't care about, give him that to use. Fill it with something heavy to prevent it from sliding about. But something attached firmly to the wall is best.

Some cats prefer to scratch objects lying on the floor. With luck and persistence, you can teach them to like just one piece of carpeting bought especially for them. Choose a doormat or something similar, so that it won't slide, and make sure that it is unlike your other carpeting.

Training the Cat to Use the Post

The training process takes two weeks or less — probably, it will only take a few days. During that time, put the post in the bathroom. You can screw it to the wood around the door, or using heavy electrician's tape you can affix it to the tile if you plan to put it elsewhere once the cat is trained. Make very sure that it is taped securely.

The bathroom is usually the only room in the house that contains nothing that could be scratched. If you have wall-to-wall carpeting in the bathroom, take it out for this short period of time. Towels, bathmats, and shower curtains are not solidly in place and are unsatisfactory for scratching because the cat can't get a real grip on them. If you have another room, such as the kitchen, which could be completely shut off and which contains nothing that the cat could scratch, you may use that if you prefer. Don't use a room which contains an object that the cat could scratch even if you don't care about that object. The whole idea is to train him to use cork (or whatever) and nothing else.

Of course, the cat's litter and fresh water should always be in the same room as the post during the period when he's going to be locked away from time to time.

Diagram 4

During the training period, lock the cat in the bathroom when you are asleep or away. In other words, when the cat is unsupervised, he's locked in a place where there's nothing but cork to scratch. When you're around, let him out but keep an eye on him. If he scratches *anything* but the post, say "BAD CAT" (or his name) and lock him in the bathroom for twenty minutes. Put his paws on the post, then lock him in, which he'll hate because he wants to be out with you—he'll cry and cry. After twenty minutes, let him out. If he's good, fine. If he scratches anything, repeat the procedure: "BAD CAT," followed by twenty minutes in the bathroom. Thus, when you're away or asleep, the cat has no choice but the post, and when you are around, you reinforce the use of the post.

Your cat is both intelligent and eager to please you. Training is simply a matter of getting it into his head. You'll know he's trained when you come home one day, open the bathroom door, and your cat runs to the post, looks to make sure you're watching, and starts scratching madly. Praise him extravagantly. He is now trained, and can be trusted to use his post from then on. He need not be locked in the bathroom anymore, and can sleep with you. You can now put the post wherever you wish.

This method works 90 percent of the time if you are consistent. You will feel mean when you hear him crying in the bathroom, but training is far kinder than declawing, and your cat's exile is only temporary.

If, after two weeks of serious, consistent effort on your part, the cat cannot be taught to stay away from the furniture, you can then declaw if you must. You can't have your furniture ruined, and if you're always angry at him for destroying your things, your anger will be just as bad for him as declawing. Most cats, however, will easily learn the rules and will love to scratch on their posts in order to win praise. My cats are true blackmailers and dash to the post whenever I'm mad at them. They're saying, "See, we're being good, so you have to praise us."

Clip the cat's nails routinely. A cat's nails get so sharp that even a perfectly trained cat can accidentally take threads out of your furniture and clothes simply by jumping on them. Also, a house cat's nails sometimes get so long that they grow into the bottom of his paws. In any case, cats are much more pleasant to have around when the claws are clipped.

You can buy a fancy clipper at a pet shop, but an ordinary toenail clipper will work just as well. Press the claw out gently. You can feel the bump at the knuckle, and press that in order to unsheath the nail. Clip halfway down— you'll usually be able to see where the vein ends and avoid that. If you do cut too far down by mistake and draw blood, don't worry—it'll just stop bleeding. In fact, that's the way most vets take blood smears from cats. The clipper must be in this relation (diagram 5) to the claw. This way (diagram 6) would split the nail. Clip the nails about every ten days.

You shouldn't have a lot of trouble clipping your cat's nails once he loves and trusts you, particularly since clipping doesn't hurt (unless you go up too far accidentally and draw blood).

Some cats, however, seem to detest it. I have a theory that it's being turned on their backs that they don't like, not the actual clipping itself. It's certainly much easier to get the paw in the right position if a cat is on his back. You can grip him with your left elbow, and use your left hand to push out the claw gently and your right hand to clip (vice versa if you're left-handed).

If your cat is giving you a hard time, try doing it the hard way. Lie on top of his back, holding his body down with your body. Take the paw and push out the nail with

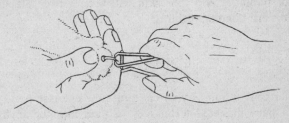

Diagram 5

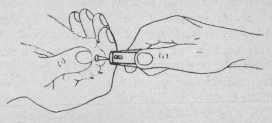

Diagram 6

your left hand, and reach around as best you can to clip from the front with your right hand. If all else fails, you can put him in his carrier and wait until he sticks a paw out of the hole or dangle something to induce him to stick it out, then grab and clip. You could also have a friend cover him with a coat or blanket and hold him while you gently pull the paw out.

I don't highly recommend either of these last two methods, particularly since they shouldn't be necessary, but if you're unsure of yourself, either will do you until you get the feel of it and can do it right. Try to get your cat when he's in a relaxed mood—perhaps having his evening siesta—and above all don't give him the impression that you're nervous yourself.

Clipping is really as easy as brushing your cat, and makes him much more pleasant to live with. Your clothes, your furniture, and your skin will benefit from the small effort that clipping requires!

DISCIPLINE

After you've trained your cat to use the exercise post, you will have mastered techniques to train him for anything else. I would recommend putting the cat in the bathroom to cure all big disciplinary problems. When I say "big," I mean the one or two, possibly three at most, problems that are really important to you. If you use this technique to punish everything, the cat will be confused. He won't grasp the idea that one particular action is a real no-no. Eventually, he will give up and resign himself to living in the bathroom, costing you the love of the cat as well as the ability to teach him manners.

Besides preventing the cat from scratching furniture, the disciplinary issue most important to me is being awakened in the middle of the night (or in the morning, if I am sleeping late). I have successfully trained every cat I've ever had to let me sleep—some within two or three days, others within a week or slightly more.

I did not start by putting the cat in the bathroom when I went to bed. Instead, I resigned myself to a few nights of being awakened so that the cat would get the idea of direct cause and effect. The minute the cat *did* wake me, however, no matter how innocently and in whatever manner, I would get up and lock him in the bathroom. I wouldn't scold or give him any attention. I'd just lock him in, go back to sleep, and let him out when I got up. After two or three nights of this, a cat will realize, "If I don't wake her up, she won't put me in the bathroom," and he'll let you sleep. If the bathroom is so near the bedroom that his crying keeps you awake, put plugs in your ears. After all, it's only for a few nights. This technique really does work. I've used it on many cats, including those of visiting friends, and it's amazing how quickly they catch on if you're consistent. I know you'll feel mean, but having good manners is best for him as well as for you.

Cats seem able to distinguish when you're really sleeping, as opposed to when you're feigning sleep. They also know what specifically woke you—whether it was meowing or rocking the bed, or whatever.

A cat banished to the bathroom will cry and cry piteously. He'll also tear all the toilet paper into little tiny pieces, so take it out ahead of time. When the cat is locked in the bathroom, give him something with your scent on it for him to curl up in and derive comfort from. By "your scent" I don't mean Chanel No. 5. I mean a nice dirty used towel, an old sweater you are through with, or a shirt that hasn't been to the laundry.

You can also set up a little behavior modification by association, something that I did by accident with my cat

Waddy. Waddy is a Tonkinese, and inherited his voice from the Siamese side of the family. We would all take turns saying, "Shut up, Waddy," when the talking became too much—with, of course, no results whatsoever.

When he started waking me with his talking, however, I'd whisper "Sshhh" to him and then put him in the bathroom. He'd cry dolefully but soon learned not to talk when I was asleep. I soon discovered that he'd be quiet whenever I whispered at him, indicating that he associated the whisper with being put in the bathroom. Of course, I would never put him in the bathroom for talking too much during the day, only for waking me. As I said, you should only use that technique for one or two really important crimes. Now Waddy understands that. He will still sometimes stop talking when I whisper, but perhaps only because the whisper calms and pleases him. Many cats love to be whispered to, and find it soothing. Others may think it sounds too much like a cat hiss and will hiss back.

Squirting a cat with a water pistol will cure him of minor infractions. Cats are so fastidious that they don't like getting their beautiful fur wet, especially not in such a sudden and undignified way. Even cats who otherwise like the feel of water still don't like being squirted. At the same time, it's not cruel and doesn't train a cat to fear your hand when you're not holding the water pistol. But for heaven's sake, don't get trigger happy! If you squirt your cat every time he annoys you, he'll become neurotic. Use it to protect a specific piece of furniture or to punish one specific naughtiness, not for anything that happens to displease you at the moment. Above all, be consistent.

If there are young children in the house, don't use a water pistol at all. A young child cannot be expected not to misuse it, neither should you.

Remember, when disciplining an animal, give him lots of love at the same time. Always praise him when he gets a lesson right. He'll understand from your tone of voice. Bad behavior is often a result of stress. Nipping, for instance, is the result of an almost uncontrollable urge. You may not be able to eliminate the cause of the stress, but you can alleviate it with love, praise, and stroking. Think of praise as a tranquilizer to be used along with the disciplinary process.

NUTRITION

I approach the subject of nutrition with trepidation because it's something most experts don't agree on. I became interested in human nutrition many years ago after reading Adele Davis's books. After having studied them, I felt I knew all I needed to know about feeding myself. Wrong! Since then, I find a new theory every time I pick up a paper. At the moment, carbohydrates are in and protein is out, at least as far as many of the experts are concerned. I've found that half the foods I thought were good for me are bad, and vice versa. This doesn't mean that I think the whole subject is nonsense. It simply remains in an exploratory stage. With experts disagreeing more and more every day, an intelligent layman can do little more than read and discuss the various points of view and then decide for himself. As new findings appear, I revise my opinions. But until all the experts agree on the perfect diet, I decide for myself which diet or combination of diets seems most reasonable.

Many people think that the experts concur far more often on animal nutrition than on human nutrition. This is true only about the kind of animal nutrition that benefits people. For example, people who raise minks are very knowledgeable indeed about what kind of diet produces beautiful fur, but that doesn't necessarily have anything to do with what will enable a mink to lead a long and healthy life surrounded by his grandchildren. Cattle farmers are very good at feeding cows in order to produce delicious steaks or lots of milk, but that has little to do with the well-being of the animal in the long run. So, we're forced back to the same old conclusion: ask what kinds of food will lead to optimum health and longevity, and they all disagree. Even less is known about this than about human nutrition.

The pet-food companies have performed extensive research on what will appeal to the animal on the grounds of smell and taste (usually chemically produced), as well as on what may be inexpensively produced and easy for the owner to pour from a box. They also try to make foods "nutritionally complete," skirting the fact that animals make use of certain nutrients in a totally different way than people.

The opinion that makes the most sense to me (which is also backed up by twenty-five years of observation) is that cats are carnivores and therefore need raw meat. We, being omnivores, can absorb and utilize food from both animal and vegetable sources, but we shouldn't expect this of our cats. One of my favorite vets in New York is a vegetarian himself and cannot bring himself to recommend meat for cats. I respect and sympathize with him, and perhaps the world would be a better place if animals did not devour each other, but that's not the way nature made it. Expecting cats to eat mostly vegetable products is like asking a horse to have a nice, juicy steak for dinner! Many cats are, in fact, eating foods of almost entirely vegetable origin (read the ingredients on a box of dry or semimoist cat food)— but at what cost to their systems? Yes, these foods have been processed so that the animal likes their taste and smell, and so that they can somehow get through his system without making him sick, but they must certainly strain a system programmed by nature to fuel itself on raw meat. I don't doubt that if it were profitable, you could process a steak in such a way that a horse could absorb it and live on it. But in the long run, the inappropriateness of such food for his digestive mechanism would tell.

So, back to raw meat. In the absence of definitive studies to the contrary, I'll go with what the animal goes for in nature. When a lioness opens up an antelope, what does she eat first? The heart, kidneys, liver—all organ meats. I recommend kidney because it's cheaper and doesn't cause diarrhea. Add plenty of calcium to balance the phosphorus in the kidney. Never feed your cat organ meat without a calcium supplement (remember that in the jungle the cat also eats the bones). So chop up the kidney, including all its fat (cats need a lot more fat than dogs), and add calcium: cottage cheese, powdered milk, bone meal from the health food store, or powdered dolomite will do. To this mixture, add any good feline mineral and vitamin supplement (powdered), some polyunsaturated oil (most vegetable oils, but not olive, palm, or cottonseed oil, are polyunsaturated), and some salt. The polyunsaturated oil helps prevent urinary calculus (not a problem with this diet, but you can't be too careful) and the salt will keep the cat drinking lots of water to flush out the kidneys. This raw mixture, or at least the meat in it, must be frozen solid for several days in order to kill any parasites. Freezing is as effective as cooking for this purpose, though it takes longer, but it does keep the meat raw—the state nature intended for the cat. Incidentally, it is impossible to can raw meat.

If you have a large freezer, you can make a big batch at one time and freeze it in individual baggies, each containing one serving size. Thus, after the initial work, it's very easy to thaw out one day's worth at a time and put it on a plate—you don't even have to open a can!

Proportions are approximate. If, for instance, you have freezer space for about fourteen servings (approximately seven days' worth for a kitten, but don't be too rigid about amounts), use four pounds of chopped kidney, including fat; one cup of plain yogurt or cottage cheese or four table-spoons of powdered calcium or dolomite; two to three tablespoons of a good vitamin mineral powder based on yeast and high in vitamin C; two tablespoons of polyunsat-urated oil; and one teaspoon of salt.

If making this mixture seems overly difficult or if you don't always have the time, don't worry too much. After all, I eat and drink a lot of things that aren't especially good for me, and I'm sure you do too. I'm not trying to make your life difficult—try to make this the basic diet but have a few boxes and cans on hand for those moments when you're not in the mood to prepare it or you have run out. There are brands that are not sold in markets, such as CD or Science Diet, which can be obtained from vets or certain pet shops and are supposed to be much better than the regular commercial varieties. Of course they're not raw meat, but they're fairly good alternatives because they don't contain tuna as do most of the commercial brands (I will discuss the problems posed by tuna shortly).

In addition to this mixture, the cat should occasionally (once or twice a week) get a raw chicken neck to chew for the sake of his teeth and gums. Cats love to play with chicken necks as well as to eat them. It can get a little messy, but it's worth the trouble. Many people are afraid of chicken bones splintering, but a neck bone doesn't splinter like a wing or back bone. Whenever you have chicken, give your cat the neck.

A raw egg yolk once or twice a week mixed with a little water is delicious and good for his coat. Never feed raw egg whites, either to the cat or to yourself, because it de-stroys an essential B vitamin, biotin. Cooked egg white is harmless, but not particularly necessary.

Always leave fresh water and remember to keep refilling the bowl. This is a must.

Quantity seems just as individual a matter for cats as for people. Some cats just require more food than others. While he's growing, give him as much as he needs. After he's grown, watch to see if he's getting fat. If he isn't, give him what he wants; if he is, cut back. Many people think that cats put on weight as a result of alteration. This is not so; the cat's metabolism slows down naturally at this point, which happens to coincide with the time for alteration.

No diet will be right for every single cat or person. If your cat seems allergic to this or any other diet, discontinue it. If he has a particular health problem that might contraindicate this diet, discontinue it. If he throws it up consistently (all cats throw up occasionally), or seems not to thrive on it, discontinue it. Some cats, for instance, are constitutionally predisposed to calcium deficiency. Not a common problem, this does occur occasionally, just as certain people are by heredity predisposed to certain ailments. Always consult your vet about special and unusual health hazards to your particular cat, and follow his advice.

If, for any reason, you must switch to a diet other than this one, I'd suggest meat or chicken rather than fish, and canned rather than dry or semi-moist food because canned food contains less ash and fillers.

If the label mysteriously lists "fish," it probably contains tuna. Cats become addicted to tuna fish, and once addicted, it's almost impossible to wean them from it. But tuna can be harmful to your cat. It seems to lead to urinary calculus in altered males.

Furthermore, tuna is deficient in vitamin E—a steady diet of tuna makes the cat irritable and overly sensitive to touch. This applies particularly to cats that have become addicted to tuna and will eat nothing else.

If your cat is a tuna addict, you must break him of his habit. Add a little bit of another food to the tuna at first, then more and more of it, until finally you eliminate the tuna entirely. At some point, the cat will catch on to what you're doing and may go on a hunger strike. If so, up the tuna portion a little, then revert to the slow elimination of it. This, combined with lots of love and stroking while the cat is eating, will usually do the trick, but it's much better never to start cats on tuna at all, cat-food companies to the contrary.

As far as mealtime is concerned, a grown cat can be fed once or twice a day, whichever works best. Do not, however, leave food out for more than twenty minutes at a time. If your cat hasn't finished in twenty minutes, pick up the food and make him wait for the next meal. The cat will be less finicky and fussy about food, and will start getting hungry because it's mealtime, just like we do. If food is available all the time, he'll get bored and picky. Also, as cats get older, they tend to sleep after eating and to eat after sleeping, so cats who constantly have food around tend to do nothing but eat, sleep, eat, sleep, and become fat and lazy.

When I say "mealtime," I don't mean a certain exact hour. Mealtime is when you get home, so don't feel guilty if one night you come home at five-thirty, feed the cat, and go out again, and on another evening you don't come home until two in the morning. He'll start salivating when he sees you. If you're not there at six, he'll just play for a while and go back to sleep.

Pooh-Bah (Pookie), a marvelous Burmese who belongs to friends, has a subtle way of letting them know it's dinnertime as far as he's concerned: he rattles his empty plastic food dish. If he thinks no one has paid sufficient attention to this, he bangs it around loudly all over the kitchen floor. He also prefers to drink from an ordinary glass at the sink, rather than from his water bowl.

If you do decide to feed only one meal a day, for your own sake I suggest that it be the evening meal. Cats expecting breakfast will wake up five minutes earlier each morning to ask for breakfast. If they aren't expecting breakfast, they'll let you sleep. Of course, you can train them as discussed in my chapter on discipline, but it's much easier on the cat if the issue never arises at all.

As your cat gets older, I suggest changing his diet to include more carbohydrates. Add wheat germ and yeast to the moist foods, serve more dry food, and use the canned prescription diets sold by vets and special pet stores, and which contain corn, grains, etc. (read the label).

With many older cats, the kidneys and the liver are the first vital organs that cease to function properly. With people, carbohydrates nourish the kidneys and, particularly, the liver. If you've ever had hepatitis and consulted a good doctor, he'll have told you to eat bread, pasta, and such to hasten the healing process, and not to worry about your weight. I realize that I seem to be contradicting myself, since I've said before that cats digest foods differently and naturally produce substances that we, being omnivores, must eat in order to obtain. If, however, you've been giving your cat mostly meat and not putting a strain on his digestion for the first ten years of his life, you're in a position to weigh one risk against another.

Obviously older cats, like older people, can and do die from many causes, but in my own experience I've heard kidney failure and jaundice cited as the cause of death so much more often than anything else that I therefore try to nourish those vulnerable organs—even without statistical evidence that this nourishment is guaranteed to help.

Whenever and whatever you choose to feed the cat, take care not to tease him. Many people, including ardent cat lovers, tease animals at feeding time. They don't intend to

be the least bit cruel, just to create a heightened anticipation. You know the tactics—holding the food dish high off
the ground and letting the cat jump up for it or meow and
rub against his owner's legs frantically before it's finally
put down. His owner might say, "Just wait a minute while I
throw the can away," or "Doesn't that smell good?" He
might also make the cat wait, for no reason, until he has
finished his own dinner before feeding him, thus forcing
the hungry cat to sit and watch as the smell and sight of
forbidden food produces unnecessary stress.

Animals take food *very* seriously. We all do, of course,
but with the exception of unusual circumstances, *we* know
when, where, and what we are going to eat, and we derive
pleasure from waiting till dinnertime and smelling the delicious odors coming from the kitchen.

A cat, however, will become quite nervous and insecure
if constantly teased and made to wait for no apparent reason. He receives the message that food will be provided at
whim and might at any time be withheld completely. No
matter how innocent your intentions, if you are whimsical
and capricious about food you will create stress that can
show up in numerous ways apparently unconnected with
food. Animals are instinctual rather than intellectual; they
know in a far deeper and more atavistic way than we how
vital food is. They have good reason: centuries of foraging
for food and avoiding starvation have heightened the animal's instinct to place food first. Animals without such a
highly developed instinct have long since died out.

If your cat seems frantic over food, especially over a
particular kind of food, think of indulging him at first.
Make sure he has a specific appetite as opposed to generalized hunger. Constant hunger in a well-fed cat is a sign of
worms. It's advisable to take a stool sample to the vet for
diagnosis.

But if every time you have chicken, for instance, the cat does handsprings even though he's just eaten, you will only make his frustration worse by denying him. For heaven's sake, give him some! A warm bone right from your plate is better than a few little pieces of chicken. He will love it, and it will keep him occupied for quite a while. Give him a thigh bone rather than a more delicate breast or end-of-drumstick bone. After a few months of being indulged in his one big food passion, he'll be content with one bone rather than three and will feel secure in the knowledge that he will be indulged when in extremis. He will gradually become less frantic, and in the end will probably lose interest in that food altogether and be more than content with the food you put down regularly for him. As I have said, animals take food seriously. Don't deny them needlessly.

Now, you won't want to try this method when guests are around. To minimize the cat's frustration, shut him in another room before anyone starts eating. If the guest or guests are old friends who like cats, you can use their presence as an opportunity for discipline. You want to make the cat understand that the begging and/or the stealing are bad, not the actual craving for the food itself. Let him stay while you're eating, as you would usually do. Make sure that he's already been fed, and is not really hungry. The minute he makes a pest of himself, put him in the bathroom and don't let him out until the meal is over (the old bathroom disciplinary treatment I have discussed before). When you let him out, give him a little of whatever he wanted. He'll get the idea quite quickly that you won't tolerate bad table manners, but that if he cooperates, you'll treat his feelings and appetites with respect.

3

YOUR CAT'S HEALTH

HEALTH PROBLEMS AND VETS

The first step in protecting your kitten's health is to inoculate him against distemper (also known as enteritis or feline panleucopenia), a viral disease that destroys white blood cells and causes extreme dehydration. This disease is swift and deadly, but fortunately easily prevented by proper vaccinations. Any good pet shop or breeder will have already inoculated your kitten, but if for some reason this hasn't been done, take him to the vet for a distemper shot immediately. Kittens not yet weaned have a natural immunity through mother's milk, but as soon as weaning begins, they should receive inoculations. With most vaccines there should be two inoculations, ten days apart, then another one when the kitten is three months old. This is especially important to know if you get the kitten under three months of age. For some reason, any inoculations given before three months are temporary, and the lasting ones cannot start before this time. Another booster at the time of alteration (seven or eight months) is a good idea. Vets suggest a yearly shot after that.

There is now a triple vaccine, one-third of which prevents distemper and two-thirds of which prevent respiratory diseases. Some vets feel the triple is absolutely necessary, some feel it can actually give the cat respiratory disease, and some feel that the distemper part is not as effective as when given separately. That's the tough part about these cases where the experts disagree. I can advise you only about the various theories so that you know what to ask and think about.

Choosing a Vet

It's almost impossible to determine whether a vet is really able or just has a good bedside manner. I hope my observations will help.

First, I would suggest that you watch out for large clinics, even those with good reputations. I know from experience that some reallly fine vets work at these places, but the drawback to all large clinics, whether for humans or animals, is that you never know who you're going to get, especially in an emergency in the middle of the night. You may get the greatest brain surgeon ever to have graduated, but you may get instead someone who flunked anatomy twelve times and whose father-in-law is on the board of directors. That's why I suggest you find an independent vet who has a very small staff. If he's conscientious and knows you well enough to be sure that you won't take advantage, he'll trust you with his home number and will be willing to work in the middle of the night in a genuine emergency.

In my efforts to keep readers from making the same painful mistakes I once did, the following may sound overly harsh on the subject of veterinarians. I neither dislike them as a group nor do I personally know any vet whom I dislike. But that is not the point. The point is that most people, even very intelligent ones, even members of the medical profession, tend to idealize vets, which is unfair to the vets themselves, and can often lead to heartbreak.

If you are a typical pet owner, you probably love your pet more than you realize. You are probably slightly ashamed (particularly if you are an American man) of admitting even to yourself just how devoted you are to this little animal that unquestioningly adores you and looks to you for all his needs. You are probably a little embarrassed by how protective you feel and how special your relationship with this small creature has become

Then the animal becomes sick. You go to the vet in a very ambivalent state. Maybe it's nothing, and you're coming across as an hysterical idiot. Maybe it *is* something, but we all know that animals are survivors, so you're probably looking pretty silly. Even if you're trying not to show it, you pin all your faith on the vet. He certainly wouldn't have picked this profession if he didn't feel about all animals the way you do about yours.

He certainly would! Vet school is harder to get into than medical school, and city vets make more money than most doctors. They also keep more civilized hours. An M.D. can charge more per case because people have insurance and animals don't, but a vet can see many more patients per hour, and at his own convenience. An M.D. must carry staggeringly heavy insurance and can be ruined professionally for negligence. Vets can't, because they are largely unsupervised and because animal-protection laws do not carry stiff penalties. The most a vet can be sued for is the purchase price of the animal. This kind of money constitutes no more than an annoyance, not a serious threat to a vet's career. Some states, such as New York, do not permit an M.D. to charge directly for lab work (blood tests, etc.) and the laboratory bills the patient directly. Vets have no such restrictions, leaving them free to rake money off the top for all lab work.

With this in mind, let's take another look at the pet owner taking his animal to the vet. It often doesn't occur to the owner that his is just another cat to the vet, that the vet may be busy that afternoon or going to a party later that evening. It doesn't cross the owner's mind that the vet has long ago calculated to the second how much his time is worth. The vet also knows that, in many cases, long hours of emergency treatment might not save the animal, and that people who say, "I don't care how much it costs" might mean it at the time, but will deeply resent it if they are presented with a huge bill. From experience, the vet knows his customers will think that if the vet really loved animals, he would stay up for two nights running, cancel all engagements, and then send a "reasonable" bill. They also will probably not pay the bill, particularly if the animal does, in fact, die.

If, on the other hand, the vet really does act like the hero that his customers assume he is, he will soon begin to resent the time, the animals, and the customers. It's a no-win situation.

Am I describing a villain? Certainly not! You and I would do the same. Vets generally end up spending the amount of time which they feel they can reasonably afford, and assure you afterward that they did all that was possible. They play the odds. A vet has learned that he's as much a hero if he cures an illness with a quick injection as if he had expended back-breaking hours for very little money. The vet concentrates on the big picture—he relies on getting the animals in and out, as many as possible per hour, for his money. He knows that a cat lover will eventually get over a cat's death, and he knows you trust him implicitly.

It's true that all good vets will, from time to time, take heroic measures for no money at all. They certainly could not do so on a day-to-day basis. It's unreasonable to expect this—yet most pet owners unconsciously and unreasonably expect exactly this heroic, saintly behavior from the first vet they find with a pleasant personality.

Be aware of the facts, and be as realistic about vets as you are about the other people with whom you do business. Be polite but aggressive when you visit the vet. Ask if 24-hour-a-day care might help your ailing cat, and if so, ask the vet to show you how to provide such care yourself. He certainly won't tell you if you don't ask—he assumes that you don't want to know. If he assigns you impossible tasks (like giving pills which your cat won't ingest, or sterilizing your entire house), call him on this.

Remember that animals, when not in the critical phase, recover more quickly and more happily at home. Beware of a vet who wants to keep your cat for days and even weeks after an illness. There may be a good reason, but don't be put off with, "He'll be less likely to get into trouble in a cage where he can be watched." Those cages simply are *not* watched in most places twenty-four hours a day. The animal, already recovering from the stress of illness, can be (and often is) pushed past his limits by the stress of separation from his favorite people and places. If necessary, bring the animal in every day so that the vet will be forced to perform hard tasks himself and argue about the bill later. If he doesn't supply a good reason for 24-hour care, consider the possibility that the vet is stumped and won't admit it.

Don't be afraid of being a pest—unless, of course, you really are one. You are probably a pest if, for many months or years, you have frequently been calling and visiting the vet for problems that always turn out to be not the least bit

serious. Most animals experience only one or two really
serious illnesses in their lives. A little education will help
you determine which symptoms are minor, and which indicate danger.

WHEN TO CONTACT THE VET

People often panic needlessly over problems that appear to
be severe but are really perfectly normal (such as vomiting)
and then neglect, through ignorance, the real warning sig-
nals. The following section, while in no way intended as a
substitute for professional medical attention, will help you
to judge when to relax, when to get alarmed, and when to
wait and see.

A really sick cat *looks* sick. He suddenly assumes a
drooping posture—head down between the paws, chin
dragging on the floor. Usually, he is also dehydrated. To
determine this, pinch the skin on the back of the cat's neck.
If it pops back into place immediately, he is not dehydrated. If, however, it stays up and recedes only gradually,
he is dehydrated. (Practice this on a healthy cat, so you can
see how the skin should go back. Then you will be able to
see the difference when you suspect dehydration.) Take
him to the vet at once.

If it's really serious—such as distemper, which is sig-
naled by dehydration and a droopy appearance—even the
first twelve hours will tell the tale. Ask the vet immediately
if it is distemper. Do not rule out this possibility because
the cat has been inoculated. There have been many cases of
bad or poorly refrigerated vaccine. If it is distemper, have
the vet do all he can right then and there, then take the cat
home and nurse him yourself through the crisis period.

Force fluids into him with a syringe. Ask the vet if you should mix the fluids with a little milk, glucose, etc. Give the cat love and attention. His chances may not be too good, but they're far better than if he were left in a cage.

Another serious illness to watch out for is urinary calculus (or UC), which most commonly attacks altered male cats. With this disease, a type of silt or sand forms in the urinary passage, leaving the cat unable to urinate. The main preventive strategy for this is diet (covered in the chapter on nutrition). The telltale sign is a cat straining at the box to urinate, with nothing coming out except perhaps a few drops of bloody urine. The cat may in desperation try to go someplace else, hoping that a change of location will relieve his suffering. Don't wait—go to the vet at once. Urinary calculus will kill within a few weeks if untreated. Insist that the vet do something that really works. Don't settle for advice to keep feeling the bladder; if you're like me, you won't be able to feel it until it's too late. Don't accept a regime of pills unless you see that they're getting down and staying down. Be sure you know what you're doing. If you don't (and you may well not), force the vet to come up with an alternative—otherwise, you'll be very sorry.

I've recently heard of another remedy for urinary calculus: adding powdered vitamin C to the cat's food. (Do not use this method as a preventative. Most cats do not get urinary calculus and, being carnivores, they manufacture vitamin C and don't need it as a dietary supplement.) If the cat has developed UC, however, vitamin C works as a medicine. The acid in the crystals dissolves the silt, stones, or whatever the blockage consists of. I've talked to many cat owners who have used this method, and they've told me that the UC never recurs, unless they forget for a time to keep adding the vitamin C.

If anything other than distemper or urinary calculus afflicts your cat—such as a virus or a respiratory infection—you don't need to rush to the vet. If, for example, your cat is sneezing or has sniffles or a runny nose and eyes, your pet shop may be able to help you if it has a meaningful health guarantee. At least you have enough time to let the shop's staff observe the cat, prescribe the obvious medication, and assess the severity of the case before scurrying to the vet.

If your vet diagnoses a serious illness like leukemia or peritonitis, ask him exactly what treatment he plans. If this consists of no more than the initial shots or other medication, followed by fluids and tender loving care, take the cat home and do it yourself. Listen carefully to the vet, but also use your own head. If he suggests total isolation (which involves a huge boarding fee), remember that air is air and can carry germs from one place to another in his place as well as yours. Your other animals have already been exposed and either will have contracted the sickness already (see the section about home care for the sick cat) or they won't get it anyway.

FATAL ILLNESSES

One of the most agonizing decisions a cat owner must make is whether to put a sick and suffering animal to sleep. Nobody has limitless amounts of money, and no one can assure you that the cat will return to health even if you spend your entire fortune trying to save him. Either way, the decision is traumatic and guilt-inducing. If the animal is extremely sick, it's truly kinder to put him to sleep than to put him through all sorts of painful tests, pokings and proddings, force feedings, etc.

There are, however, exceptions. One of the ways to judge your vet is by the advice he offers in the case of a very sick cat. If the animal is jaundiced or acutely anemic, his prognosis is poor, and a good vet will advise euthanasia rather than make the animal suffer needlessly. You can detect signs of these ailments yourself by looking at the inside of the ears, the roof of the mouth, the mucous membranes on the underside of the cat's eyelids and in the spot where the eyeball meets the eyesocket. If these areas are yellow or dead white instead of pink, the illness is probably serious. You should go along with your vet if he strongly suggests that treatment will be useless and that the cat will be better off if put to death humanely.

With many other kinds of serious illnesses, the animal has a reasonably good chance of recovering and living to a ripe old age if the vet is willing to expend a lot of time and trouble. Distemper, for instance, can often be cured if the vet will work for several hours through the crisis period. A cat can also be saved from urinary calculus, even if the bladder is swollen to three times the normal size, but the vet must spend long and painstaking hours of very slow, on-and-off catheterization of the animal. Many vets are unwilling to devote so many hours to one patient because they can make more money by taking several patients for ten minutes at a time. Also, if the animal dies, which may be a fifty-fifty probability, the vet knows that the owner will resent doubly a sizable bill.

If the second a vet sees a sick cat he suggests that the animal be euthanized without further ado, seek another opinion. If the vet says that the chances are so slim that an expensive work-up is not worthwhile, find out what he means by expensive. If he means only that he's not going to work for hours and hours unless he's sure it will be well worth his time, he's not for you. There are illnesses that *do* require expensive lab tests, operations, transfusions, dialysis, and the like, but if the vet mutters vaguely about lab tests when the cat is already in crisis, translate this as unwillingness to be bothered. The results of the tests won't be in for several days, by which time the cat will have died. Look for a vet willing to take time. If you're on the lookout, you'll be able to detect if you're being rushed through, however charmingly.

A cat can be expected to live fifteen to sixteen years, although I've seen cats as old as twenty-three, and I've heard of still older ones. As with people, however, life expectancy is very individual, so you really have no way of knowing if your cat will die older or younger than the average.

Don't try to prolong the life of the cat if he is obviously ready to go. A friend of mine had a cat who was dying and she just couldn't handle it. She repeatedly took Gigi to the vet for steroid shots which helped temporarily but which were only postponing the inevitable. Finally, the vet told my friend that she was being selfish, that the cat was suffering needlessly and should be euthanized.

After my friend had done this, she told me that she had known all along that Gigi had been begging her with her eyes and her moans to be left to die without pills, injections, and proddings—her time had come and she knew it.

Minor Health Problems and Needs From A to Z

Baths

Normally, you should never have to give your cat a bath. They keep themselves clean, and bathing only removes necessary oils from the fur and skin.

Nevertheless, some extraordinary event may force you

to bathe a cat. The first time he came to my house, Pooh-Bah, the cat of friends of mine, managed to upset an entire can of grease all over himself. Without a bath he could never have licked it all off, and it would have made his fur rancid and sticky—not to mention that the grease would have rubbed off on everything in the house.

If you must bathe the cat, prepare everything before mentioning it to the cat. Fill the bathtub with clear, lukewarm water cat-shoulder-deep. Fill the kitchen sink with lukewarm water cat-shoulder-deep and add dishwashing detergent (much easier to rinse off thoroughly). Have towels ready and windows closed to prevent drafts. If possible close off the kitchen-bathroom area from the rest of the house.

When all is ready, pick the cat up gently and get him into the sink before he even knows what's going on. Washing him thoroughly shouldn't take long at this point. Then quickly put him into the bathtub, rinse him, and wrap him in a towel to absorb the moisture. He'll lick himself dry fairly quickly, but be sure to keep him out of drafts until he's dry.

Cerebellar Hypoplasia

Cats sometimes suffer from another syndrome, easily mistaken for calcium deficiency, but which actually stems from minor brain damage, called cerebellar hypoplasia, wherein the cat lacks a certain amount of coordination. If your cat happens to have this (it's relatively common, occurring in approximately one out of ten thousand cats), do not panic at the phrase "brain damage." The cat will have the same good health and life expectancy of other cats. He has a minor motor impairment that mostly affects the hind quarters. The cat may be more liable to topple over when going at high speeds, and may at times be wobbly and weak in the hind legs. This in no way affects his intelligence and disposition and is unlikely to make any difference to you.

Cats with cerebellar hypoplasia are also financial bargains, since they are less salable. Some pet shops even put them to sleep, but only because they do not want the expense of feeding and caring for an animal that will not bring top dollar.

Constipation

Constipation occurs rarely and is almost always temporary, and emotional in origin. Consult your vet only after you've ruled out emotional factors and are sure the problem is not just temporary. Again, watch for droopiness and listlessness, and also examine his anus. Sometimes a long-haired cat will become blocked on the outside by dried feces and you must remove the hard mass carefully with warm water and a little detergent. Work slowly; remember that the area by now is painful, and the mass must be softened with care before being removed.

A stool expander and softener for people marketed under the name Siblin (there are also other brands such as Metamucil) helps cats as well. In fact, some vets repackage it in their own bottles under their own prescription labels and sell it as a laxative and as a remedy for hair balls. Mix it into the cat's food. It expands in the stomach and bowel and generally rids the cat of blockage. However, sometimes a cat may become internally blocked and need surgery. Again, consult your vet.

Dental Care

Cats have tooth and gum problems just as we do. And, as with people, susceptibility to these problems varies widely from cat to cat.

It is easy to see when a cat has a sudden sharp pain in his mouth, such as we would get from a cold blast on a cavity. He will take a bite of food, leap away, shake his head vigorously, and refuse to touch that particular food served on that particular dish in that particular place.

My friend's cat, Elsa, got a sudden sharp pain while eating dry food. She was fine after she went to the vet and had her teeth cleaned, but for weeks she would eat dry food only if she first brushed it all off the plate and scattered it all over the floor. The association was clear: food from that dish meant trouble. Her tooth wasn't the problem, Elsa figured, that dish hurt her tooth.

The cleaning process is the same as with people, except that for obvious reasons the cat must be anesthetized so the vet can work on the mouth.

Generalized pain in the mouth from gum trouble is less easy to spot. Take a look at the cat's gums from time to time, particularly when he's an older cat. If they are red and spongy instead of pink and smooth (as with people), the cat may need to have his gums and teeth cleaned and scraped. If the cat won't eat but hangs over his food as if he'd like to eat, a sore mouth could very well be the reason.

Examine his mouth carefully. See if you can find a splinter or something lodged in the gum. Smell his breath —bad breath could indicate bad teeth. Even if you can't find anything, take him to the vet. The cat might have a hairline crack in his tooth, or something wedged so deep that you can't see it, or it might even be tartar under his gums.

Most vets can treat dental problems easily. It's important that your cat's mouth be treated if necessary. An infected mouth can infect the whole body and make your cat very sick indeed.

Diarrhea

If your cat gets diarrhea, just change his diet a little. Add more cottage cheese or anything binding like cooked rice, and experiment with the formula. Anything that is binding for people is binding for a cat. You may also add dolomite to the food, which works very well.

Milk will often give a cat diarrhea. This can be a problem, particularly if you have a cat who likes and tolerates milk, and you then get a new kitten who develops diarrhea from it. Milk is unnecessary, and you shouldn't have gotten your cat hooked on it in the first place. But if you can't keep the kitten away from the older cat's dish, and don't want to subject your first cat to additional stress—the new kitten as well as his favorite drink being withheld—give them cream instead. The cream is practically pure butterfat —like liquid butter—and contains almost none of whatever is in milk that causes diarrhea. The cream is expensive but will solve the problem, and the extra fat is good for the cats, unless they are very overweight. You can also water down the cream to the consistency of milk, thus letting your cat think he's still getting his favorite drink.

Ear mites

If the cat seems to be scratching his ears a lot, look inside. If his ears look dirty, it could just be dirt or he could have mites. There are ear-mite medicines on the market, or your vet can give you some. Since you can't easily distinguish dirt from mites, you might as well act on the assumption that the cat has mites and clean the ears accordingly. There are ear-mite medicines that you may have to get from a vet if home remedies don't seem to last, but you can certainly start on your own and hope that you won't have to bother with a vet. One of our breeders told me of an unusual remedy for mites that works well for her—boric acid powder. Get a box of cotton swabs—the kind with wooden sticks, not the plastic ones which bend easily. Dip the cotton in water and then in the boric acid powder, and insert it in the cat's ear and dig out the brown deposit. This will take many cotton swabs for each ear— just keep digging until they come up clean. Don't be afraid of digging too deep. The inside of the ear curls around before getting to the eardrum, so you can't ram into the eardrum by accident.

If you are fairly certain that it is dirt and not mites, you could use mineral oil or just water, but boric acid won't hurt, particularly if you wipe out the residue of boric acid with a tissue from the part of the ear that is exposed, so that it could be licked by another cat or gotten at by the cat's own paw. Remove it with a tissue inserted as far as your finger can reach.

Fleas

Examine the cat's coat periodically, especially if he seems to be scratching often. If he has fleas, you will be able to see either the fleas or flea dirt, which looks like flecks of black pepper. If your cat's fur is so dark as to mask the flea dirt, set him on a large piece of white paper and brush, shake, and fluff his fur. Any flea dirt will show up on the paper.

If your cat does have fleas, give him a flea bath—one that can be rinsed off—or have the vet give him a flea dip. If he doesn't have fleas, do not take preventive measures. Flea collars are toxic—that's how they kill fleas—and cats often make themselves mildly sick by chewing such collars in attempts to get them off. Furthermore, these collars often cause a rash around the neck, hidden to the owner by all that fur but nevertheless there. Flea powder causes the same problem: it's toxic and the cat will lick it off.

Fungus

Fungus is not as serious as a lot of vets make it out to be. It's easily cured by a series of pills, although the fur takes a few months to grow back. If you see even a small, hairless scaly patch, take the cat to the vet. If the cat has a fungus, five days of pills, plus an iodine bath, should kill it. Give yourself a strong soap or iodine bath too. There are also some effective new creams and lotions available which can be used either with or instead of the pills.

Hair Balls

Since cats lick themselves constantly to keep clean, they get a lot of fur in their stomachs, and from time to time develop hair balls. Often cats throw up in order to empty their stomachs of hair. Sometimes, however, they try and try to throw up to get rid of the hair, but they can't quite bring it up. If this happens you will notice a certain kind of retching, usually with the shoulders hunched up and the head moving compulsively straight in and out, strange squeaky noises, and nothing coming out except a little clear liquid.

Several products on the market are designed for this problem, but plain vaseline is just as effective and much cheaper. Put a dollop of vaseline about the size of a lima bean on the roof of the cat's mouth so that he has to swallow it. This may be a bit messy and he may struggle a little, but he'll get most of it down. Do this two or three times daily for several days. The vaseline will bind the hair in his stomach and he'll then be able to get rid of it, either by vomiting or excreting it. If he's prone to develop hair balls, you can also give him a little vaseline twice a week even when he's not having the problem.

Refusing to Eat

If your cat won't eat, consider the possibility that his teeth and gums may be hurting (see the section on dental care). But if this does not seem to be the case, keep in mind that although many people worry if their cats won't eat, it's perfectly normal, even for a cat that has always been a good eater, to go off his feed from time to time.

At first, take up the food as usual after twenty minutes, and make him wait until the next feeding. If this continues for two or three days with no other signs of illness (such as droopiness), try tempting him with goodies to see if he's just bored with the same old stuff. Try baby food, shrimp, canned crab meat, breast of chicken—anything. If he's still not eating, and particularly if he's listless and droopy, take him to the vet. But if he does eat, you know that he's being finicky. In that case, make mealtimes quite regular for a while—remember that mealtime means when you come home or get up—but then feed him immediately. Don't wait. On no account leave food down between meals. Soon he'll begin to feel hungry at his regular mealtime, just as we do.

Runny Eyes

Almost no kitten escapes having runny eyes at some point in his development. This is usually temporary and does not necessarily indicate an eye infection. A red, swollen eye is infected, however, and may require a trip to the vet. But first, bathe the eye twice a day with a boric acid solution. If this doesn't work, then take him to the vet.

A merely runny eye with no other symptoms, however, can be treated with boric acid quite effectively until the cat outgrows it, which can take as long as a year or more. Runny eyes are a mild allergic reaction and do not require major treatment. So why let your cat take medicine needlessly? Let his eyes run a little.

Because they have pushed-in noses and therefore very small tear ducts, Persians are especially prone to this problem, and may require an eye-wash of some sort for many months. On a white or light-colored cat, the discharge shows up as a dark stain on the fur around and under the eyes. This looks terrible, but if you know what it is and why it happens, you can stop worrying and simply keep washing the cat's eyes.

Boric acid can be purchased as a solution or in powder form and then made into a solution according to the directions on the bottle (the same solution for cats as for people). The powder is cheaper but the solution spares you the task of boiling water. Warm the solution a little for the comfort of the animal.

Sneezing

When a cat or kitten first enters a new house, expect him to sneeze for a few days. A dry sneeze means that the cat is getting used to new dust, a mild allergic reaction that will go away after a few days. A wet sneeze with mucus coming out of the nose and eyes means a cold, and possibly requires a trip to the vet if the cat doesn't seem to be getting better after a day or two.

Toxoplasmosis

This is an internal parasite, cured by a series of pills. It might not seem to merit special attention, because if your cat seems sick, you would take him to the vet anyway, where it would be diagnosed by a stool sample or blood test, or both, and treated by the vet.

But two vets to whom I spoke have such different attitudes to toxoplasmosis (coccidiosis) that this seems a perfect example of "Which vet do you believe?" One of them considers it a terrible health hazard (to people) and leans toward euthanizing the cat in the interest of the public safety. The other said, "Oh, I've had toxo hundreds of times—it's no worse than having a slight cold."

I feel that unless you're in the habit of cleaning out the litter box with your bare hands and then licking your fingers, your sick cat poses no more danger to you than the millions of homeless street cats wandering around who undoubtedly have this and many other diseases. If you are so susceptible that you contract toxoplasmosis from any stray that comes anywhere near you, you're not safe anyway. If you're not, you won't get if from your own cat if you are minimally clean and careful. I have worked for over ten years with cats, including cats that have had toxo, and have never contacted it (or if I have, my case was so mild that I never knew it).

This holds for a lot of other diseases considered extremely communicable from cat to cat. It seems that people and animals are immune at most times to most diseases, particularly those diseases that have been around constantly for a long time. If this were not so, all of us who use public transportation, or even walk in city streets, would be sick constantly.

Worms

In the initial stage, a cat with worms eats ravenously without gaining weight. I am not talking about a normal, good appetite—I mean almost frantic eating and constant hunger, with the cat remaining quite thin. In the later stages, he becomes droopy and often won't eat at all.

If you suspect that your cat has worms, take a stool sample to the vet for analysis. Worms are cured by pills, usually administered by the vet and necessitating that the cat stay at the vet for a few days. There's no reason you can't administer the pills yourself if you prefer, but you'll have to keep the cat in the bathroom for a few days because he'll have diarrhea. Most vets won't allow home treatment, however, unless you insist.

HOME CARE

Giving Pills

If you have to give your cat a pill, the least traumatic way for all concerned is to grind it up and mix it with his food. Be sure to put it into only a little bit of food and watch him eat that before giving him the rest of his dinner.

This method works if:

1. The pill *can* be ground up.
2. The cat isn't so sick that he's not eating anyway.
3. The pill doesn't make the food taste so bad that the cat won't touch it.

If you can't use this method, you must get your cat to swallow the pill. Hold the cat's body firmly next to your own, with your heads facing the same direction, with your left arm and elbow (vice versa if you're left-handed) and tilt his head back with your left hand. Open his mouth by pressing between the canines and the molars with the thumb and middle finger of your left hand. Quickly drop the pill into his mouth with your right hand. Then close the mouth with your left hand, keeping the head tilted (but not so far back as to force his swallowing mechanism to double back on itself), and stroke his throat gently with your right hand until he licks his nose (diagram 7). *If he doesn't lick his nose he hasn't swallowed the pill.* He has tucked the

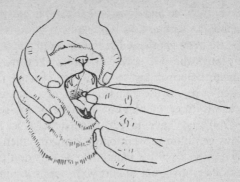

Diagram 7

pill in his cheek and is willing to wait forever for you to turn your back so that he can spit it out. If he hasn't licked his nose after a minute or two, you'll have to start over. If he dribbles or foams at the mouth, let him spit it out, wipe his chin, and wait an hour to start again. Do not panic if he foams at the mouth when given medication. This can look quite frightening, but it doesn't mean that the cat is in danger, and the foaming will stop.

This method works if:

1. You both get used to the routine so that he does swallow the pill fairly quickly, and
2. He doesn't become so upset that he throws it up.

A third method uses the same technique described above for holding the cat. Use your second or third finger (whichever is easiest for you) to push the pill down into his throat. You have to stick your finger down far enough so that you feel the actual swallowing mechanism working on your finger—the throat is contracting on your finger and hence on the pill.

This method works remarkably well with a lot of cats. It

is very quick and is over before the cat knows what is happening so that he's less likely to get upset and throw it up. Be very gentle and reassuring right up until you actually push the pill down his throat. You may even wait a minute before doing so, as if you wanted just to cuddle. Afterward, release him immediately, and the minute he licks his nose, tell him how good he is. Praise him lavishly.

You may have to get someone else to hold his front paws gently to prevent him from using them to keep your hand away from his mouth. Some cats don't do this at all, but others do—not to hurt you, but as a purely instinctive reaction, just as we put our hands to our faces or vulnerable parts of our bodies when frightened or to ward off danger.

You can coat certain pills with butter or oil to make them easier to swallow. However, they will also be more likely to slither out of your fingers, so take your choice.

If you simply can't get him to swallow the pill by any method, or if he throws it up consistently, you will have to consult your vet. Perhaps he can give you a water-soluble version of the medication that can be melted and inserted into the side of the cat's mouth by using a syringe (with, of course, the needle removed—diagram 8). Put the syringe between his lips at the side of his mouth and slowly force in the fluid. If you insert it at the front of the mouth, or if you press too quickly, the medicine could get into the windpipe or lungs instead of the stomach (diagram 9).

If you have to see the vet because your cat is not swallowing or keeping down the pills despite your best efforts, don't let the vet make you feel that you're clumsy or a nuisance, and that it's therefore your fault, not his, if your cat dies. By now you will have learned to distinguish the important problems from the unimportant. If you haven't nagged about unimportant issues, don't be afraid of being insistent about the important ones.

Diagram 8

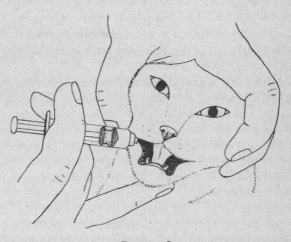

Diagram 9

You can also always discuss your cat's medications with your own personal doctor. An M.D. often knows more than a vet about the different forms available for a given medication.

Isolation

I have read in cat-care manuals and heard from vets that some cats should be isolated from the others. For instance, if you find that one of your cats is leukemia positive (leukemia is present in the bloodstream although the cat is perfectly well and does not actually have leukemia itself), you must arrange for it to have living quarters separate from your other cats. I wonder what kind of palaces these advisers live in. Is Mrs. Danvers supposed to send one of the footmen over to the East Wing to feed and to change litter?

This suggestion is akin to those vets who tell you to clean and sterilize everything in the house that your cat has touched after he has had certain types of illness. They usually tell you this in a nice, authoritarian manner, with the implication that it's quite easy and routine. In fact, this task is utterly impossible.

When I still regarded vets as authority figures, I always replied, "Yes, yes, of course," but when I got home and actually looked around, I would be numbed by the enormity of the task. When I called the vet to say, "But the cat has been everywhere! He's touched the blankets, the sheets, the quilts, the curtains, the upholstery—everything," he would respond, "Do the best you can—at least scrub the litter box."

By the time your cat has gone to the vet and been diagnosed, the damage has already been done. Your other cat has already been exposed and his fate is in the lap of the gods. Even if you have a house large enough to isolate the cat, what kind of life is that for either of you? Do you scrub up when going between one part of the house and the other?

People who make this type of impossible suggestion do a great deal of harm, even if unintentionally. Such advice protects the giver because he knows you can't do it and therefore will blame only yourself and not him if the cat dies. Nevertheless, conscientious people try frantically to carry out these suggestions, inevitably fail, and then either get rid of both cats or live with guilt and fear.

Usually—and I do mean *most of the time*—nothing bad happens if you neither scrub nor isolate, and you will quickly forget the whole uproar. The second cat has already developed a natural immunity, and if something bad does happen, it would have happened anyway.

First Aid

The single most important thing I can tell you about first aid is to have the name, address, and phone number of a vet or animal hospital that has services available twenty-four hours a day, seven days a week. Avoid huge clinics if possible, but certainly use them if there's nothing else available rather than try to cope yourself. Believe me, if you walk in and find your cat out cold from poison, electric shock, or whatever, having a plan of action—someone to call, someplace to go—will be far better than frantically leafing through the pages of this or any other book in order to discover how to perform artificial respiration or induce vomiting. Don't forget that you'll be in something of a state of shock yourself and will be doing something you've never done before. Also, you're not necessarily going to know what type of poison was swallowed or what type of burn was sustained.

So, be prepared. Discuss with your vet what happens if you call his service and he's away for the weekend. Have in mind who to call and where to go.

For the record, however, here is a brief list of emergency first-aid suggestions:

BURNS
Wash the burned area with a solution of bicarbonate of soda, then apply grease, oil, or vaseline. If the burn is very bad, don't apply grease (which keeps the heat in)—rush to the vet.

CHEMICAL BURNS

Wash with a solution of bicarbonate of soda if the chemical was an acid; a solution of vinegar if the chemical was an alkali such as lime.

POISONING

Induce vomiting (see the end of this section), and give the antidote described on the label of whatever poison was swallowed, if known; then rush to the vet.

ELECTRIC SHOCK

Apply artificial respiration (see end of this section), then put a drop of brandy or other stimulus on the cat's tongue. Don't force him to swallow.

If he's in shock from having bitten through or touched an electric cord, don't touch the cat before you unplug the cord, or you will get a shock yourself.

CONVULSIONS

Do nothing till the convulsions cease, then rush the cat to the vet.

SWALLOWED OBJECTS

If the cat is choking pick him up by the hind legs and shake him lightly. If the swallowed object is obvious—half in the mouth as well as the throat—try to remove it gently with the fingers. If it's down too far or doesn't come out easily, don't try—your vet has special equipment for doing this. Once the object has actually been swallowed, it should certainly be removed, but you have time to get to the vet and need not rush frantically.

If the cat has swallowed a string, *don't try to pull it out*. The end of the string is inside the cat and possibly curled around an organ. Take the cat to the vet immediately.

HEAT STROKE
Apply cold, wet towels to his body and rush to the vet.

BLEEDING
Press the opening from which the cat is bleeding until you
can get to the vet.

BITES
Drop hydrogen peroxide into the wound, then apply mer-
curochrome.

DROWNING
Hold the cat upside down to let the water drain out of the
lungs and pull the tongue out as far as possible. Squeeze
the water out of his lungs by pressing the cat's chest with
your hands. Apply artificial respiration, then spill brandy
into the corner of the mouth. Wrap the cat in blankets and
take him to the vet.

ARTIFICIAL RESPIRATION
For a cat that is unconscious and not breathing but still has
a heartbeat: lay him on his right side and gently pull the
tongue out—it will hang out of his mouth. Using both
hands, one on top of the other, press firmly on the rib cage
twenty to thirty times a minute. Continue till the breathing
resumes. If there's another person present, have him blow
into the cat's nose while you press the rib cage.

INDUCING VOMITING
With a syringe, slowly, and from the side, force the cat to
swallow any of these emetics:

    hydrogen peroxide solution
    one tablespoon of mustard powder dissolved in one
        cup of warm water

one teaspoon of table salt dissolved in one cup of
   warm water
one-half teaspoon of bicarbonate of soda dissolved in
   one cup of warm water

4

UNDERSTANDING
YOUR
CAT

NOT USING THE BOX

Occasionally a cat will stop using his box. This is most unusual, but it can happen. Don't panic. First determine whether the cause is physical or emotional.

Physical Causes

1. A cat developing a urinary blockage or infection will strain at the box and then try other places in desperation. Take him to the vet *immediately*. Blockage is a deadly killer. The cat needs expert medical treatment and a change of diet (see chapters on health and diet).

2. An unaltered male cat will spray. So, on occasion, will an unaltered female (see chapter on neutering). Your cat should have been altered anyway, but perhaps this territorial spraying will finally convince you to have this operation performed. The operation is perfectly safe at any age, so don't hesitate because you fear that it's too late to alter the cat.

3. Sometimes an altered male cat will still spray. He may be a cryptorchid—a cat with an undescended testicle. This occurs in approximately one in every thousand male cats. Often if a testicle is sill inside the cat's body and hasn't come down, the vet will remove only the testicle that has descended. Sometimes this works successfully, but sometimes the testicle inside continues to function and the cat is, in effect, unaltered.

   If you acquired an already neutered male that unaccountably begins to spray, ask your vet to check if the cat is a cryptorchid. Or ask the previous owner for the name of the vet who did the operation and ask him to check his records.

   Check with your own vet, of course, if you yourself bring the cat in for alteration. If your cat is a cryptorchid, insist that the vet go inside and remove the other testicle.

4. If you are using green chlorophyll litter, stop. Use regular clay litter. If you have changed brands, go back to the old one.

5. Make sure the box is very clean. Provide two clean boxes near each other to see if the cat prefers it that way. For example, place one under the wash basin and one in the tub.

   Some cats are really finicky. Some friends of mine have a cat named Bushmill who likes to wipe her paws on a towel after using the box. They kept wondering why the towels were always on the floor. Then they caught her at it, and provided her with her own towel which they taped securely to the towel rack. Bushmill now daintily reaches up and wipes her paws after going to the bathroom.

6. If your cat has started using the bathtub instead
    of his box, leave an inch of water in the tub, or
    try putting the box in the tub. Or you can just
    live with it, since the tub is easy to clean.

7. Make sure the box is not in the middle of traffic.
    If it's in a small bathroom with adults, dogs, and
    children going in and out all the time, at least
    put the box in the tub and draw the shower cur-
    tain. In other words, make sure the cat has as
    much peace and privacy as possible.

8. Some European-made rugs are tanned with uric
    acid. You can't smell it but the cat can. If your
    cat sprays on just one rug, and this rug might
    possibly have been tanned in Europe, speak to a
    cleaner about deodorizing it, or get rid of it.

9. If a cat has urinated in one spot, he will tend to
    go back to it because of the smell. Clean the spot
    with the most powerful cleaner you can find and
    keep it sprinkled with a powdered rug deodor-
    ant.

10. Long-haired cats are more prone to lose litter
    training than short-haired cats, although this
    problem does not occur often. If you've tried all
    else and failed, clip or shave the cat—it seems
    to work. Perhaps having all that fuzz between
    him and the outside world puts the cat slightly
    out of touch. The hair will grow back faster than
    you imagine, so don't worry that you will per-
    manently disfigure your pet.

Emotional Causes

If a cat is emotionally upset, he will sometimes stop
using the box. He does so partly to punish you and partly

to tell you something. In many cases you can probably figure out why he's upset, but many people don't know that change of any kind upsets cats. If someone moves in or out, the cat will hate it. If you change apartments, the cat will hate it. Even if you rearrange the furniture, the cat won't like it. Of course, I am not suggesting that every time you do anything new, the cat will automatically lose his box-training. On the contrary, this problem is very unusual. But if it should happen, consider that the cat may be reacting to a major change. Has you son or daughter gone away to school? Have you gotten married? Have you gotten divorced? Have you moved?

Obviously, you can't restore the previous state of affairs, but if you understand the problem you'll be in a better position to help your cat. Give him lots of love, but at the same time let him know that his behavior is not acceptable. If necessary, keep him in the bathroom for a while when you cannot supervise him. Use the water pistol if you catch him in the act. Praise him extravagantly when he uses the box. Keep the box extra clean. You might even give him several different boxes in different parts of the house for a while until he adjusts to the change.

If you know that a change is about to occur, bear in mind that the cat will be upset. Give him extra love and attention in advance. Moving time, for instance, is so frantic that you probably will tend to ignore the cat, and he'll be confused and hurt. Try to make a little time for him— stroke him and tell him you love him. If you are really frantic, board him at a kennel for a few days and be ready to spend time with him when he comes home.

SNIFFING

Some people find it slightly indecent that cats sniff each other's bottoms when first introduced. It is neither dirty nor indecent; it is merely cat etiquette—a cat's way of getting acquainted and learning all about the other cat. A cat will do this, incidentally, throughout his entire relationship with another cat, just to make sure that the other really is his old friend and that he hasn't changed. Sniffing tells the cat how his friend is feeling.

Cats also have a disconcerting habit of smelling your breath first thing in the morning, before you've had a chance to brush your teeth. Again, your cat is checking you out. A cat's nose tells him most of the things he needs to know about his environment and the creatures who inhabit it. Don't worry about germs—cats clean themselves from nose to bottom.

BITING AND NIPPING

Some cats, no matter how gently treated as kittens, make a bad habit of nipping. A nip is only a love bite, but it can hurt. Use the water pistol to break this habit, even if you have to carry the pistol around with you for a few days. During this time, don't use it for any other disciplinary problem. Every time he nips, say, "NO," then squirt.

At about age five or five-and-a-half months, kittens are teething. They really need something to chew, so give it to them; a raw chicken neck is ideal, a rabbit's foot is fine. Also, watch out for electrical cords during this period. But don't worry, this period won't last long.

You won't always notice when the kitten is teething. Kittens don't get holes in their mouths, like children. Rather, one tooth grows in behind the other, then the first falls out. You will be able to see these double teeth if you look closely in the cat's mouth.

Nursing

Some cats nurse on the end of their tails, on another cat, or, sometimes, on your clothing. I see no great harm in this, but if it bothers you, get some bitter apple from the drugstore and put in on whatever he's nursing. If he persists, let him. It's probably a deep psychological need arising from not having had enough nursing as a kitten.

Frenzy

All cats will occasionally seem to go crazy and run around and around in a wonderfully frenzied way. Don't worry, this behavior is perfectly natural. Enjoy it — it's really marvelous to watch.

Shedding

Your cat will shed during certain periods more than others. These are the periods when the days are getting longer or shorter more rapidly than usual. These periods are roughly from mid-February to mid-April and from mid-August to mid-October. In these periods, nature is revving up for big changes, and animals and plants change correspondingly.

Another factor in shedding and also in overall health is a cat's fondness to hot radiators and/or hot pipes. It's almost impossible to keep some cats from curling up around these very hot objects. He won't hurt himself if he curls up near them, but if he likes to be right on top of them, he could injure himself in many ways, and will certainly shed too much. If your cat has this problem, put some padding (old newspapers, for example) on the radiator, or wrap a thick towel around the heat pipe. Put things on top of the television—a book, a clock, a cable box, or a heavy ornament. Not only does the warmth of the set affect cats in the same way as other sources of heat, but some people believe that enough radiation is exuded to cause cancer in a cat that lies directly on top of the set.

Shedding can also be emotional in origin. A cat under stress will always shed more than if not under stress. If he hates being in a car (many cats do), expect more shedding. Traveling in general will often make a cat nervous. So if he seems to be shedding more, consider the time of year, exposure to heat, and stress. You can't do anything about the first, but you probably can eliminate the other two causes.

PRIVACY AND BELLS

Cats love privacy. Let them have it, or a version of it that makes them feel secure. In the first place, don't put a bell on a cat's collar. A colleague of mine used to say that the only cats that he had seen who proved after autopsy to have ulcers were cats forced to wear bells. You might argue that you want to be able to find the cat; maybe you panic if he seems to have disappeared, and you'd like to hear that reassuring tinkle. Well, that noise will reassure you but will drive the cat crazy.

You can easily prevent the problem of the disappearing cat by noticing his favorite hiding places. Cats can find the most amazing places. You can look everywhere possible, under and into everything with a flashlight, and just when you've decided he must have gotten out, he'll turn up.

You should know his favorite hiding place in case of an emergency, but once you've found it, don't let him know —give him the happy feeling of having his own secret. Don't grab him and pull him out for no reason. He'll just find another spot, and when you really do have to catch that plane, he'll have disappeared.

Some people want to put bells on their cats in order to protect birds. But your cat shouldn't be out at all. Furthermore, planning to save the birds at the expense of the cat's sanity is a kind of attempt to play God, which we humans love to do, and which usually has unexpected and disappointing results.

PUZZLING BEHAVIOR

If you have two or more cats that have always loved each other and one is suddenly, unexpectedly, and for no apparent reason attacked and rejected by the others, first try to figure out if the victim has a new scent on him that the attacker dislikes. Has he been in contact with other animals which the attacker has not? Has he gotten out? If anything like this has happened, the first cat could be attacking the smell, not the cat. Take a towel with your familiar scent on it and thoroughly rub the attacked. Then rub your hands all over him. This should make him smell okay and reassure the attacker.

If the behavior persists, you might consider taking the victim to the vet. Cats sense far sooner than we the presence of disease and illness. They will recognize it long before the illness shows up in ways that are obvious to us. Animals always reject illness—not necessarily the creature with the illness so much as the actual illness itself. If you take a clue from your cat, you might well spot the problem before it's too late.

I do not know whether a cat will react in this way to a person incubating an illness. I think not. When my own cats sense illness or sorrow in human beings, they react in exactly the opposite way. They want to comfort and be with the person.

GAMES AND PLAY

One of the most surprising things about cats is that they invent the games they want you to play with them. Dogs will learn the games you teach them, but each cat will teach you his own favorite game.

My first cat liked to play "I'll put my paw on the edge of the sofa and you try to grab it before I pull it away— then you put your hand on the edge and see if I can grab it before you can take it away." This was a game that had never occurred to me. Fooling around with the cat and paying attention to him enabled him to push me into it. He invented the game, which excited and thrilled him more than any other. Of course, he cheated when he became excited and would end up jumping over the arm of the sofa, but the game was absolutely wonderful to him. I've tried it with other cats but they've never been interested.

My second cat liked "fetch." She would jump in the air like a dog to catch something in her mouth, and then bring it back. She also would retrieve.

My third cat likes "come and chase me and be very fierce when you catch me." He'll run from chair to sofa to bed, getting caught each time before running to the next place.

My fourth cat likes "I'll steal something from you." He especially likes bag ties, and every time I take a tie from a loaf of bread, for example, he steals it the minute I put it down. I've learned to let him do this, since he enjoys it so much, and I keep an ample supply of ties.

I know that many people would say not to let a cat have ties because he might swallow one or hurt himself. This kind of generalization is useless. In this case, ties are strictly toys for my cat, who wouldn't dream of doing anything except throwing them up in the air, pouncing on them, stalking them, and stealing them. My other cats show no interest in these ties, and I'm not in the least afraid of injury.

Obviously, ties *could* be eaten and be damaging in other ways, but that's why you have to know your cats. I will explain elsewhere that cat-proofing your house is impossible (see the section on cat-proofing the home), so don't remove objects just because they might possibly be harmful. First, see what the cat wants to do with an object and whether it's going to become a favorite toy, and then decide.

Similarly, many cats love big paper bags from grocery stores. A cat will hide in one and lurk for hours, jump out and pounce, then return and lurk some more. Many cats feel very deprived without at least one paper bag around at all times. If yours is like that, give one to him.

CATS AND DOGS AND CAT PEOPLE

A psychiatrist friend theorizes that if there's a difference between "dog people" and "cat people," it's that dog people tend to be less secure and need a slavishly devoted animal rather than an independent, loving pet. I don't buy this, particularly since this doctor herself has owned and loved dogs as well as cats. I think most people are either animal people or not. If they love animals, they will love dogs, cats, cows, horses. If not, they won't particularly like either cats or dogs.

Although you may love cats and dogs equally, I want to emphasize that your initial approach with a cat will have to be different than that with a dog. Even the most loving, devoted, "bred for disposition" cat will have to be allowed to do things his way at first. If he wants to take his time exploring and getting the feel of the house before he decides to come to you and make friends, you will only put him off by grabbing and petting him before he's ready. Children especially, who will want to hold the kitty all the time, must understand that if they play hard-to-get, the kitty *will* be in their laps all the time, but this has to be the kitty's idea.

This attitude can be overdone, of course, and often is by doting cat people. They are so enchanted that the cat initiates play, and tells them which particular game to play— butting or nipping when he wants attention—that they turn the cat into a spoiled brat. Those demanding little nips are not hostile—they're a way of communicating—but they hurt, and there's no reason to put up with them. Certainly no one else will, and someday you might need to have your cat a welcome guest at a friend's house. Say "NO." Squirt with the water pistol, even tap him lightly on the top of the head if necessary. Again, use this technique only for this one problem until it disappears, and then don't tap his head at all for a while, otherwise the cat will be permanently afraid of having his head touched.

5

YOUR CAT
AND
YOUR HOME

CATS AND YOUR HOME

I strongly suggest that your cat be a house cat, not an inside and outside cat. I urge you to apply this to all cats —not just highly bred ones—even if you live in the country.

Many cats that run loose in the country are struck and killed by cars. Even if your house lies far from a road, the cat can find it. The cat can also eat grass, plants, and flowers covered with pesticides. My neighbor's cat was never quite well after sniffing too much of a spray with an arsenic base.

People also will steal cats. Some thieves just want a particular cat or think him valuable, and others sell cats to laboratories.

Finally, cats that don't even know that there *is* an outdoors are perfectly happy. Lords of the manor, they love their own good homes. Cats are true conservatives and don't like change. They like the status to remain *quo* and will not miss the outside in the least.

I know that all cats try to run out of an open door—my own apartment cats love to do this though there's nothing outside but a rare, boring small hall. It's just a game to them, another form of play, and they feel very clever if they've outwitted me and sneaked through without my having noticed. This is also an expression of the proverbial curiosity of the cat, not of some terrible longing to be out, unless your cat's not altered.

I let my cats go out into the front hall because it's not dangerous. I've trained them with the water pistol not to use the back door, which leads down a stairwell, and they never do. You can do the same with all of your doors if you live in a house.

CAT-PROOFING THE HOME

Totally cat-proofing your home is impossible, just as living a totally risk-free existence is impossible. You don't need me to tell you that swallowing a pin will be bad for your cat, but you also don't need me to tell you that advice like "You can always realize that you've dropped a pin and can always find it and pick it up" is also impossible to follow.

People die from choking on pieces of food in restaurants; people die when taxicabs go out of control and climb the sidewalk; people die from flower pots falling on their heads. Though accidents happen, normal people routinely go about the business of living and don't stay in their apartments with the shades down for fear of possible harm. Yet some of these people conduct elaborate worry sessions about protecting their animals from all eventualities. It is true that if your cat is locked in the bathroom all day it is protected against the possibility of chewing a wire and electrocuting himself. It is true that your cat might possibly choke on food that hasn't been pureed into mush. It is also true that the animal prefers a more varied and interesting life, risks and all. If you deprive him of this, you are thinking of yourself, not the cat. I could write a hundred pages of things that might possibly be harmful, but I won't. These things just don't usually happen. They are the exceptions, not the rules. And the one thing I omitted would be the thing to befall your cat.

However, you *should* watch out for a few things:

1. Don't leave windows wide open unless they have screens. It's untrue that cats never fall or jump out of windows, and it's equally untrue that they always land on their feet. Cats like window ledges and they don't have good depth perception. A gust of wind can blow a cat away, or a pigeon flying by can prove irresistible.

   Inexpensive little screens that slide to fit different-sized windows can be gotten at the ten-cent store. You can put two screens together in a very wide window. The screens stay anchored by the grooves on the side of the window and by the window itself as it meets the top of the screen. If you have casement windows, you'll probably have to spend more money and get some professional help, but this particular danger is so real that you really should do it. Don't leave windows open wide even at the top. Cats are very good jumpers and very curious.

2. Make yourself aware of refrigerators, washers, dryers, and incinerators. A cat will run out of the apartment, see an open incinerator, and jump in out of curiosity. A cat will jump unnoticed into the refrigerator—he knows where the food is. A cat will settle down in the nice warm laundry left in the dryer, snuggling in so far that he can't be seen. Someone comes along, decides the laundry isn't quite dry, shuts the door, and turns the ma-

chine on again. I've heard sad stories.

3. Make a habit of being observant. Feel the cat from time to time; under that fur things can be felt but not seen. Look into his mouth. Something could be wedged into his teeth and gums and cause infection. Examine his paws. Be aware of unusual behavior such as grumpiness or moodiness, things that might indicate pain.

4. A very nice treat for a cat is a dessicated liver pill or a yeast pill from the health food store. Cats love these pills and they are very good for them. But you must then be aware of other pills. If your cat sees anything that looks like his favorite pill, he will grab it. If you put down an aspirin (deadly to cats) for just an instant, he will gobble it. The difference in color is not noticeable to him, nor can he detect a particular smell.

This applies to all other pills. If you take a lot of medication, don't reward him with pills as treats.

PLANTS

To keep cats from eating your plants, make a mild solution of hot pepper sauce and water, and spray it on the leaves and petals. It doesn't harm the plant, but it tastes bad to the cat.

If the dirt around the plant attracts your cat, sprinkle the dirt with bay leaves or orange peel or both. These two scents seem to repel cats.

Some plants are poisonous to cats—philodendrons and poinsettias are those most commonly found in the house. The general rule is that anything toxic to people will be toxic to your cat. If he does eat a philodendron leaf, he will throw it up—not always in time to keep from being sick, but as least in time to keep him from dying.

PESTICIDES

Insects, particularly roaches, are often a problem in the city, but you can eliminate them even though you have cats. I use a professional exterminator, and my cats are fine. The exterminator had me shut the cats in the bathroom with the window open during the whole process and for three hours afterward, while the place aired out. He said that the bathroom didn't need exterminating and, for reasons unknown to me, he was quite right. Don't worry that your cats will think they are being punished. The presence of the exterminator will signal to them that something unusual is taking place and the cats will actually want to be out of the way.

If your bathroom window is too small for a screen, leave it open only slightly. If your bathroom doesn't have a window, discuss this with the exterminator. If he feels the slightest doubt, board your cats elsewhere for the day. If you live in a building like mine, where the building management has keys to all the apartments and where the building's regular monthly exterminator might be allowed to enter in and squirt during your absence, make *very* sure that everyone in the building understands that this is not to happen EVER. If necessary, leave a note on the door on the day the exterminator makes his rounds.

If you do the exterminating yourself, read the label on the product. If it says, "Harmless to household pets," feel free to use it, particularly if you shut the cats in the bathroom and air out afterward. If you don't have a powerful window fan to speed the airing, allow more time. If you use boric acid to kill roaches, be sure not to sprinkle it at random but inside cracks, inside the stove (under the metal tops that cover the burners), behind sinks and the stove, and inside closed cabinets. This method also works perfectly for me.

Some of my customers swear by the high-frequency sound devices that make noises that bugs hate but domestic animals and humans can't hear. A friend of mine, however, tried one. When it didn't work at all, he was told that these devices have to perfectly adjusted to be effective. Since the manufacturer was in Florida and my friend was in New York, since he didn't know how to adjust it, and since it takes weeks before you can determine if the adjustment is correct, he found the device impractical and forgot about it. Besides, how can you be sure that cats can't hear it, not to mention be irritated and driven crazy by it, particularly after you've been fooling around with adjustments on a do-it-yourself, hit-or-miss basis for weeks and weeks?

NOISE

If you live with a lot of noise, you'll have to be especially tolerant of your pet. Nature created animals for a far quieter universe than the one in which we exist. Loud, harsh, and mechanically amplified noises produce a great deal of stress in animals.

Human beings who cope well with stress brought on by loud sounds are usually the ones who consciously and deliberately choose to listen to them. But anyone forced day after day to listen to too many unwanted decibels will become edgy and irritable, or worse. Animals have even less tolerance for loud noise.

I find that people who habitually express themselves at the top of their lungs and very vocal people who are temperamental (without being neurotic) are often very attractive to other people and to animals. They often have a lot of charisma, and are truly good to—and for—people and animals. Yet their noisiness is stressful to their animals, particularly on a long-term, daily basis. For their animals, these people are the whole world. The animals adore them and are happy with them, but their noise is still stressful.

This pertains twice as much to people who are professional musicians and who practice at home. I don't mean the person in a symphony orchestra, who uses no mechanical amplification. I mean my many charming clients whose art depends partly on mechanical amplification of sound (electric guitars, electric anything), which takes a heavy toll on the animal. I also mean people who usually play radios or recording devices very loudly.

Please don't misunderstand me. I am not suggesting that you give up either animals or decibels. Merely be aware that if the animal exhibits symptoms such as wheezing, sneezing, asthma, diarrhea, or anything that *could* be psychosomatic, they probably *are* psychosomatic and can therefore be overcome.

Before rushing to the vet, try a three-day period of silence—quiet voices, no yelling, no amplified music, and lots of love. If the animal stops exhibiting the symptoms, you will then know what caused them. Gradually reintroduce louder sounds, but slowly and with lots of reassurance. If you make this effort, you will soon have an animal who is as tolerant of noise as you are, and you two will live happily ever after.

REPAIRMEN

Be very careful when expecting repairmen, delivery men, or anyone who will be coming in and out of your home.

Either keep the cat in your arms, or preferably, shut the cat in the bathroom or bedroom, away from the activity if there's to be a lot of coming and going.

The greatest danger is someone's slamming the door on the cat accidentally or letting a self-closing or screen door shut on the cat. As a cat owner, you have become conscious of such dangers, but you can't expect this of others and you won't be able to provide constant supervision, particularly if you have repairmen coming in and out many times an hour. I myself have heard of several cats whose backs were broken in these circumstances.

A second danger is that the cat will get out. I've already discussed how easily cats do this and how quickly they can streak past you.

A third danger is that the cat will become upset by all this new activity, and have an accident on the rug or throw up.

6

YOUR CAT
AND
YOUR FAMILY

NEW BABY

People often ask me if a cat will be jealous of a new baby. He won't once he figures out what the baby is, but the entrance of this strange little creature into the house will confuse the cat. He's pretty sure it's not another cat, he's pretty sure that it's not a dog, but it *certainly* isn't a human being—it just doesn't smell and look right. He'll do his big hissing number so that this potentially dangerous animal will know not to mess with a tough guy like him. In other words, the cat is scared, and if you realize this, you'll be able to handle the situation. Once he's finally figured out that the baby is a human kitten, he'll be perfectly wonderful and infinitely patient, putting up with having his tail grabbed or being dressed in doll clothes— behavior he wouldn't allow in a grown-up for a minute! In fact, when the baby gets to the active stage, you should protect the cat from *him*, not vice versa. A two-year-old, no matter how kind and intelligent, can't be expected to realize that an animal isn't a toy. It's never too early to teach a child kindness in the same way that you teach him to brush his teeth—by constant repetition.

Young Children

Parents will often get an animal in order to teach their children responsibility. They will say that the child can have a pet only if he takes care of it. This is fine, if not carried to extremes. If the child learns to exert himself for something he loves, he is learning something very valuable, but always remember that the parent must take ultimate responsibility. If you allow the child's neglect to cause suffering, you are teaching him only to be a callous human being, not a responsible one. If you punish him for forgetting his responsibilities, you will teach him only to hate the animal and to feel guilty—two very bad emotions to instill in an impressionable child. But if you yourself make sure that the animal is fed, watered, cared-for, and loved when the child forgets, and you make sure that the child is praised when he remembers, you will make the world a better place and the child a better person.

Allergies

Most people who are allergic to cats will be allergic to some but not to others. As far as I can see, allergies are unrelated to the length or quality of the hair; most people feel that the dander (sloughed-off skin) causes the trouble. However, according to Dr. Charles Schaubhut, a New York veterinarian, the latest theory is that it's not the hair or dander that triggers the allergic reaction, but the saliva that becomes attached to the hair. In keeping with his theory, Dr. Schaubhut recommends that the cat be brushed with a soft brush and wiped with a damp towel to remove the saliva. In addition, he recommends rinsing the animal every two weeks with a solution of one tablespoon of fabric softener to one quart of water in order to render the coat nonstatic.

Allergies are not related to breeds—a person can be allergic to one cat but not to another in the same litter. So, if you have allergies and want a cat, try holding different ones until you find the one that doesn't make you swell up or otherwise react. There are, of course, shots for this as well as for other allergies. These shots are effective and should be borne in mind.

A well-known New York vet is allergic to cats, yet he must treat them all the time. He keeps air purifiers in every room of his office and that, with anti-allergy shots, seems to solve the problem for him.

Two of my friends control their allergies with vitamins, one with vitamin A, the other with vitamin C. Experiment prudently and under your doctor's supervision. You might be pleasantly surprised!

Furthermore, some customers have told me about a kind of lotion found at health-food stores. I haven't tried this myself, but my customers say that when rubbed into the cat's fur, it keeps allergy-causing dander from getting into the air and that it works miraculously. Of course, the cat looks a little different—a bit plastered down—but the lotion, I'm told, doesn't harm upholstery.

Finally, many doctors will tell an allergic patient to get rid of his cat without determining whether the cat is indeed causing the allergy, so be positive that it's the cat and nothing but the cat before resorting to such a drastic measure. There's no reason to deprive yourself of the joys of owning a cat even if you have had allergies to other people's cats.

IF FAMILIARITY BREEDS CONTEMPT

There will come a time—maybe not this year, maybe not until five years from now—when you will begin to resent changing the cat box. By that time you will have become so spoiled that you'll have forgotten how easy it is to care for a cat—how you don't have to walk it, you don't have to worry about its crying when you're away, you don't have to do much of anything. You accept the cat's love, but think it almost too much to have to change water every now and then, put down food every now and then, and mostly, keep the box clean.

Don't let yourself resent your responsibility. Changing the box can be a bore, but it's nothing compared to the trouble you go through with any other animal. Stop and think of how much love, affection, and cleanliness you get from such easy work.

GETTING A SECOND CAT

I think having two cats is ideal for both you and your cat. Some people choose not to get a second cat because they want and need all of a cat's attention. One of my friends admitted that she knew her cat was desperately lonely. She herself, however, was going through a bad time and she was unwilling to give up the cat's wild demonstrations of relief every time she came home. She was away all day and most evenings (she would often work until midnight and be in the office again at eight in the morning). She knew the cat sat and pined all day, bored and miserable, but she couldn't do without the almost hysterical reception she got at home.

I know that you don't exist just to give your cat pleasure, but the cat doesn't exist just to give you pleasure either. As with all other relationships, yours must be mutual, or the pleasure mysteriously evaporates. Had my friend not finally gotten a second cat, her first would have one day given up, become dulled by boredom, and finally forgotten how to play and even how to love.

This won't happen if you really are home most of the time and are willing to be the animal's constant companion. But if, like most of us, you are not home the best part of every evening, your cat probably needs a companion. Don't fear competition for the first cat's affection. Both cats will relate to you, particularly if you acquired them a few months apart. They will keep their *joie de vivre* and your absence will not make them quirky, neurotic, or dulled.

Incidentally, an only dog needs company even more than does an only cat. Cats sleep a lot during the day, but a dog feels abandoned and cries, even if you are out only for a few hours. A cat is a very good companion for a dog and vice versa.

Having two cats, as I said, is ideal. Many people prefer to have three, four, or more cats. Like me, these people become irresistibly attracted to an animal after they have decided not to bring home any more. They fall in love with cats.

If you want to have a lot of cats, be sure you can provide enough space for all of them, and that there are not too many other cats for each cat to cope with psychologically. Studies show that animals (and humans) become neurotic when overcrowded—don't upset the ecological balance.

Introducing a New Cat Into a One-Cat Household

When you adopt a new cat or kitten, expect jealousy. It's absolutely natural, and it won't last. Even though your first cat needs a playmate and will be happier in the long run, he'll be furious at first and will show it. After all, it's his house and his territory; the new cat is an interloper and has no business there. If you can, pretend to ignore the new cat, and lavish affection on the old one. Tell him how much you love him and that he'll always come first with you; he'll understand from your tone of voice. The new cat will not notice. He's too busy with new observations and is not expecting any particular kind of attention at first.

Above all, don't interfere. Don't try to be a referee. You'll only make things worse if you say, "You bad cat, how can you be so mean to that sweet little kitten?" It's best to go to the movies, and leave them alone to work it out. You'll be afraid the first cat will harm the second, but he won't. He'll act very fierce and he'll scare the new-comer to death, but he won't actually harm him. In a few days or less, he won't be able to resist playing with the new cat, and they'll end up fast friends. In fact, he'll be much happier after the initial adjustment period than he was as an only cat.

Your first cat will also be healthier with a second cat to groom him and clean the insides of his ears. An only cat can't provide this care for himself, but it is part of cat love.

As with all generalizations, there are exceptions to my prediction that two cats will quickly become friends. Sometimes the first cat, particularly if he's much older and a gentle soul, will go into a decline instead of fighting. If this happens, and the first cat's depression seems to endanger his health, give back the kitten and wait until the older cat dies. You have waited too long to give your cat a companion.

On the other hand, it's better not to get two kittens at the same time. You will avoid filling one cat with jealousy, but you run the risk that the two cats will relate to each other and not to you. Get the second cat after the first is well trained and has been there a few months. The first cat will teach the second the rules of the house, and they'll both relate to you.

Incidentally, the relative size and age of the cats has nothing to do with determining which will eventually end up "top cat." A cat doesn't know that he's bigger or smaller than that other guy. The issue of "top cat" always seems to hinge on a mysterious personality trait; not on questions of size and strength.

7

TRAVELING WITH
OR WITHOUT
YOUR CAT

IF YOU HAVE TO LEAVE YOUR CATS

If you are taking a trip, what should you do about your cats? If you're going only for a weekend, you can get away with leaving them plenty of food and several containers of water (in case they accidentally upset one). Many people are fearful of leaving their cats, but after all, you leave your cat alone much of the day anyway. A freak accident could happen while you were out shopping for an hour just as well as it could happen over the weekend.

People often ask if they should take along the cat if they go away for weekends. If you go to the same place every weekend or during the summer weekends, take the cat. The trip will soon become routine instead of change; the cat will see this as the place he goes every weekend with his favorite people.

If, on the other hand, you visit different people every weekend, he'd probably be better off at home or boarding, depending on the length of your stay. New people and new surroundings are definitely not a cat's idea of fun.

If you are away for a long period of time—on a vacation or a business trip—the best solution, if you can manage it, is to have someone stay in your apartment during

your absence. Being in his own home with familiar surroundings gives a cat security, so even though he will miss
you, he will be spared the double jeopardy of missing both
you and his own home.

Unfortunately, this is usually not a workable solution.
The friends whom you trust have their own lives and are
probably unwilling to move into your house. And it isn't
safe to hand a key to a relative stranger, no matter how
pleasant he or she seems.

The second-best solution is to give your cat to a cat-
loving friend while you are away. For a period of more
than four days, simply having someone come to feed and
change the litter once a day is not enough. The cat will
become very lonely and depressed. If he goes to someone
else's house, he will have a bad first few days of adjustment, but then will be happier than if left alone.

This too can be difficult to arrange. Many people simply
don't have friends who would be delighted to take in cats
for a long period of time. And, of course, the person must
be carefully picked. He or she must be a true cat-lover,
preferably a cat owner himself, and must not regard cat-
sitting as an imposition and a chore.

Boarding

The last alternative, and for many people the only alternative, is boarding. When selecting a boarding kennel, try
to look at the place not from your point of view, but from
the point of view of the cat. Chicness and expensiveness
are rarely the best criteria. A cute little menu with restau-
rantlike descriptions of various delicacies may reassure
you, but means nothing to the cat. No matter how well
equipped, a fancy private room is, in effect, an isolation
ward. The cat would much rather feel safe and secure in a
smaller, protected space where he is able to see what's

going on. Remember that it's very easy, even with the best intentions, to neglect an animal stashed in an isolated place. People get busy, and the cat can go for hours with an empty water dish or a claw caught in something, struggling to get free.

Look for a place where the boarding animals are not upstairs, downstairs, or somewhere in the back. Ideally, they should be out where everything is going on. This means that every customer will, in a sense, be looking after your cat. A customer will notice and point out an empty water dish or a bad eye which the person in charge might not have noticed for hours. The cat may also observe the comings and goings, the people, and the other cats, but from a safe and secure spot, his own private and inviolable enclosure.

Incidentally, don't put him in a place where all the cats run around together. This inevitably leads to the spread of disease—and believe me, even one cat incubating disease can spread it. Furthermore, a cat without a place of his own often feels threatened by all those other animals.

Also make sure that your cat will be in a section for cats only, secluded from the barking of dogs or the threatening presence of other strange and unknown animals.

IF YOUR CAT IS GOING WITH YOU

Air Travel

Most airlines will allow one pet per passenger class to travel with the owner, on a first-come, first-served basis. With this in mind, make your reservations early. Check with the airline as to the type and size of carrier required —usually you must have one that fits under the seat. Since these are very small, bring a collar and leash so the cat can sit on your lap for most of the trip; usually no one will object.

If you must ship a cat, check as to what type of carrier each individual airline requires and what procedures are necessary. Most airlines do not require a reservation, but want you to have the cat there two hours before the flight. Some require a health certificate, some do not. If the temperature is below 45 or above 85 degrees at either the departure or arrival point, most airlines will not ship the cat.

You might also consider what some airlines call "priority parcel" (some have different terms for this service). Under this plan, the cat (in his carrier) goes with the regular passenger luggage rather than with the freight. The advantage is that the cat doesn't have to wait in the cargo depot for two hours before being brought over to the hangar for pick-up, but comes right down with the passenger luggage. For this reason, the rules on temperature usually don't apply. This service costs a little more and must be prepaid, but the advantages, both for you and the cat, far outweigh the liabilities.

When your cat must be in his traveling case for quite a while, especially when traveling by air in the baggage compartment, put a small tin of ice as well as a small cardboard box of litter in the carrier. As the cat licks it, the ice melts slowly but won't spill all over everything.

Car Travel

Some cats travel very well in cars, staying away from the driver, happily looking out the window or sleeping. Others are dangerous if not in a carrier or on a collar and leash if a second person is in the car. They want to explore the brake and the accelerator or distract the driver. To find out whether your cat can be trained to stay away from the driver's area, experiment in a lot or field, keeping the windows closed, of course, except for a crack. If you have the kind of windows that open and close mechanically with a button, be especially careful. It's hard to imagine a cat being able to open or close such a window accidentally, but it's possible.

Whether in or out of the carrier, if the trip is longer than two or three hours you will need a small cardboard box of litter and a tin of ice (as described in the section on air travel).

If you are stopping en route at a hotel or motel, be extremely careful. Even if the hotel management permits a cat in the room, it's dangerous, but if you've sneaked the cat into the room it's even more so. A maid with a passkey comes in to clean and the cat is out the door like a shot. Find out from the maid what time she'll be coming so that you know when to put the cat in his carrier. Leave the "do not disturb" sign out whenever you're not there.

TRANQUILIZERS

I do not recommend tranquilizing a cat. I understand that some vets recommend tranquilizers, particularly valium, if the animal is under stress—as when taking a long plane trip. M.D.s, however, have long referred to a bad reaction to tranquilizers as the "cat reaction." The cat will panic at the feeling of going under and losing control. Instead of inducing a nice calm state, tranquilizers can produce exactly the opposite effect. The cat fights and fights the tranquilizer until it either wears off or knocks him out totally. Doses so heavy that they almost immobilize the cat are dangerous because of possible bad effects on metabolism and breathing. The cat must be carefully confined and monitored until the reaction wears off, which sometimes requires days. Wobbliness hits the back legs first and leaves them last, so the cat may reel around for days, sometimes forever.

I know that vets who do recommend tranquilizers say that given in *precisely* the right dosage, such medicine is okay, but that's the trouble. Cats, like people, vary widely in their reactions to all types of drugs. That's why the biggest risk in any operation is an adverse reaction to the anesthetic. What will barely affect one person will literally kill another. Vets do not have highly trained anesthesiologists on their staffs; they themselves anesthetize, and are usually quite careful, but playing around with delicate variations in dosages when not absolutely necessary is really asking for trouble. It's better to go ahead, let the cat be upset, and calm him later with love and attention. Cats are remarkable realists, and sooner or later will realize that what can't be cured must be endured, and will settle down and go to sleep.

General Hints

I'm sure you have noticed that cats love to use absolutely clean litter. This can even be annoying: you get the feeling that the cat can't wait to jump in and dirty the litter the minute you've cleaned it, that he's been waiting for his big chance. Why couldn't he have used it before you cleaned it, so that the nice new stuff would stay cleaner longer? Well, that's just the way cats are—they are clean animals and drawn to clean litter. You can use this to your advantage when traveling. Wait until just before you leave, then clean the box and change the litter. Chances are good that he'll rush to use it the minute you put it down and will therefore be able to start the trip with an empty bladder and/or bowel.

If the cat hates traveling and has hidden the minute he realized that a trip is imminent (cats can always tell), put down the clean litter before you start packing, getting out bags, or signaling a trip in any way, and then pack as quickly as possible after he's used his box.

8

FINAL
PARTINGS

ABANDONMENT

Millions of cats and dogs are abandoned at the end of every summer. People either buy or take in pets for the summer because it's nice to have an animal in a vacation home. The weather is good, the lifestyle easy and less complicated than in the winter, and caring for an animal may be difficult in the city, but a cinch in the country. Usually, at the very beginning of the summer, the cat a person takes in is also very young and cute and cuddly. By the end of the summer, the pet will soon need to be neutered if he hasn't already started spraying (or going into heat) and looking for a mate.

Because of this, and because such people really did want the animal only for the summer, they decide to abandon the animal. I imagine that these people rationalize that they've given the animal a good start in life; that without them he wouldn't even have had that one good summer; that he's no worse off—and, in fact, better off—for having been with them for the summer; that he'll be able to fend for himself now that he's had this good start; and that someone else—some year-round resident—will adopt him.

I beg you not to be one of those people! These animals, accustomed to depending on humans, are pitifully unable to fend for themselves. They haven't learned the art of survival and are ill-equipped to learn it at such a late date. With winter approaching and millions of other animals having been similarly dumped, the crammed shelters don't begin to have room for the animal, and he is condemned to a slow, miserable death.

Please do not amuse yourself with a summer pet if you aren't willling or able to give the animal a permanent place in your life. If you live in the country and an obviously well-cared-for animal comes to your door, take him in and try to find the owner. Call the local newspaper, the police department, and the local animal shelter. Most communities have a bulletin board someplace—the local supermarket, for instance. If an owner is looking for his pet, he will have called the same places and put up a notice himself.

An abandoned cat came to me one Labor Day weekend. She was so sweet and so used to beds, laps, and cuddling, that I was sure someone must be looking for her. Of course, I had no luck finding the owner, and the nearest shelter was inundated with strays and had no room. So I brought the cat back to the city, had her altered and inoculated at my own expense, and put her up for adoption.

I realize this is asking a lot, but most cities have very inexpensive spay/neuter clinics, and your local vet can often find a home for an attractive animal. If you cannot place a stray, it costs about five to ten dollars, depending on where you live, to have the animal euthanized humanely, which is certainly preferable to leaving him to starve slowly.

WHEN YOU CAN'T KEEP A CAT

If, for some reason, you can no longer keep a grown cat, you may have a problem on your hands. If you and the cat are lucky, some friend of yours will have gotten to know and love him, and will be happy to take him. This is the ideal solution. If you aren't this lucky, ask around the neighborhood, put up notices in your building, approach friends at work, and put an ad in your local paper. If these methods fail, call various animal shelters. If one has an opening, it will take your cat and put him up for adoption. Often, however, these shelters have waiting lists since they are usually overcrowded, and they usually will charge a small fee or request a donation.

If you have tried everything without success, I'm afraid the only humane recourse is to have the cat put to sleep by a veterinarian. This is a quick, painless procedure, and your cat can die peacefully, in the arms of his favorite person, and never know what happened. I know that you will find this solution intolerable, and I'd give anything to know of a better one. But I don't. Paying someone to take him might save your conscience, but won't do the cat any good. The person who takes him only for money will probably have no qualms about abandoning him as soon as your back is turned.

There is also quite a flourishing little business in selling animals to labs for experimentation. Beware of strangers who don't appear to be animal lovers but who are willing to take a cat off your hands. If you have any doubt, make the person pay at least twenty-five dollars. For this very reason, all humane organizations charge an adoption fee larger than the rates paid by labs. Also, people often place more value on something for which they have paid than for that which is free, and consequently will tend to treat the animal better. If you feel bad about making money this way, donate it to an animal charity—they can all use the money.

Above all, don't turn your cat loose, even in the country. He has never learned to care for himself, and will die of starvation—or worse.

If you do find someone to take the cat, tell the new owner everything you can think of—good and bad—about the animal. If you've found anything about him to be a problem, you're doing him no favor by lying in order to get him a home. The new owners will resent not having been told, and not being as attached to him as you, are less likely to tolerate a problem.

Remember also that what is a problem for one person may not be for another. A cat who will awaken a very light sleeper will not disturb a heavy sleeper or an early-morning person. Some cats will do better as country cats than as city cats, for any number of reasons—being highly active, meowing often, making great messes. We all can't stand certain things—a best friend might hate something which doesn't bother us at all. If your personality doesn't jibe with a cat's, a friend might think him marvelous. Many people, for example, want a very docile, quiet cat, while others want an active, boisterous one. So don't assume a lie is necessary. On the contrary, this is the very worst thing you can do for the animal.

Above all, keep in touch with the new owner at the beginning. Make him promise to let you know if the arrangement isn't working out. Call a few times to see how things are going. If the new owners are the right kind of people, they'll value the cat more because of your obvious love for him.

Another thing you must consider, particularly if you are older, is what will happen to your pet(s) if you die. It's not enough to leave instructions with your lawyer, for many lawyers will ignore them. Give a trusted friend a signed letter naming him "cutodian" of the cat(s) as well as putting your wishes in your will. My own inclination would be to instruct this friend to have the animal(s) euthanized humanely, particularly if they are older and set in their ways. Also make sure that the friend agrees with you and finds this proper and unobjectionable. If he or someone he knows *really* wants your cat(s), that's ideal. Otherwise, it's best to insure that they will not be made to suffer because of your death.

WHEN YOUR CAT DIES

Usually your cat is at the vet's when it dies. The vet will have facilities for the disposal of the body—unless you wish to attend to that yourself. There are, for example, pet cemeteries, and although I myself would not find that route more comforting, many people do.

If your cat dies at home, you can call the vet and ask if you can bring the body in. He will understand your feelings and will be glad to help.

COPING WITH GRIEF

For whatever help this may give you, I'd like to tell you about my own feelings of grief upon the death of a well-loved cat, and my own theory about grief in general.

I've had one cat, one dog, and three people extremely close to me die in my lifetime, and the initial grief is *exactly* the same. I think that all people have a grief meter, and that there is a limit to the extent of the grief you are able to experience (without a certain cut-off point you'd go mad or die). The ultimate limit is about as ghastly as anything imaginable.

After the first shock, you cry a lot—if you're lucky enough to be able to cry. Then you have small periods, lasting two or three minutes at first, when you actually forget, then the pain hits you again. The intervals between waves of grief gradually get longer and longer. Sometimes you'll wake up from a good dream and your grief might not hit you for ten minutes. It almost seems to switch on and off: pow/forget, pow/forget, pow/forget.

The death of a deeply loved animal taxes your upper limit just as much as the death of a person. It's not that you loved the person less than the cat. It's just that when you've hit your maximum, there's nowhere left to go.

The most helpful observation I can tell you is that the grief does not last nearly as long with an animal. Only a certain number of things will remind you of a cat—I know, there are plenty, but they recur in relation to the same places, the same things, the same times. With a person, the reminders are far more complex and far more numerous. It usually takes at least a year to get over the death of a person, but mercifully, far less for an animal.

COPING WITH GUILT

Guilt is another emotion that everyone seems to feel when a well-loved animal dies. There is always the feeling that you should have done something else—not gone on that trip; taken him to the vet sooner; let him die at home instead of among strangers. There's always something you can think of that you should or shouldn't have done, and worst of all, it's often true. There really *was* something you did wrong and you realize it now with the awful clarity of hindsight.

I have seen that it's the people who took the best care of a cat and loved him the most who feel the most guilt, whatever they did. But if you've done what you thought was best or right at the time, you have done the most anyone can do. Try not to regret having done what was right.

Don't be shocked or frightened when you find that your pain or guilt at the death of an animal is as bad as when a parent died. On the other hand, do take hope that your sorrow cannot possibly last anywhere near as long.

REPLACING THE CAT THAT HAS DIED

When your cat dies, you will have to decide whether to get another cat, and if so, what kind. Many people decide initially never to get another—partly because they don't think that they could stand to go through the grief again, partly because they fear being disloyal to the dead cat, and partly because they feel that no other cat could possibly replace the one that has died.

After a suitable period of mourning (the amount of time will vary from person to person), most people find that getting a new kitten gives them a new lease on life. They are often sure that this won't happen, and can't believe it until it does happen; but I've seen many cases like this, and never have I seen even one person who wasn't really glad that he finally went ahead and got a new kitten. Once you're a cat lover, you're a cat lover. Even if you think that only that particular cat got to you, you're wrong. You now love cats, and there's no reason to deprive yourself emotionally. Remember that it's a compliment to the animal that died if you get another.

As to the kind of cat, it's pretty much accepted in the animal business that you shouldn't get the same breed. The sad truth is that you *cannot* replace the pet that died. He had a special personality all his own, and no other cat will be the same, nor should you expect one to be. So, if you choose a pet for his physical resemblance, you will be more tempted to make invidious comparisons. If you get one that looks a little different, you will be more likely to accept that he's as wonderful as your last cat, but in a different way. This generalization makes sense to me, but like all generalizations it's not without exceptions, and you can best judge your own personality.

EPILOGUE

I hope and believe that when you get a cat you'll find that you've added a new dimension to your life and another angle from which to view the world. Numerous articles have come out lately attesting to the therapeutic value of pets, but those of us who are pet owners have already sensed that this was so. In relating to a different kind of creature, you automatically deepen your sense of self and understand better your unique place in the universe.

There's a common fallacy that if you have affection for an animal you will have less for human beings. But love is not like slicing a pie—if you give a slice to a cat it doesn't mean you'll have less left for people. On the contrary, every time you look at your pet with real love in your heart, you make a more loving person—a person with more, not less, love to give to your mate, your children, and your friends.

APPENDIX

WELL-KNOWN BREEDS

SHORT-HAIRED CATS

Siamese

The Siamese is the most popular of all the shorthairs. He is loving, active, intelligent, and playful—a perfect all-around cat. At one time, many people thought of them as jumpy and irritable. Whether this was once true I don't know, but it certainly isn't now (unless, of course, you get one from kitten mills which tend to overprocess all cats, including the Siamese).

The Siamese will take over your house and make his presence felt more fully than any of the other breeds, not just because of his very distinctive voice—which some people love and which drives others crazy—but because he's quite active, inquisitive, and able to make known his needs and wants. Once he decides he wants to be in your lap, nothing will keep him off—he'll jump up again and again, and if disciplined, will spend the rest of the evening figuring out how to sneak onto your lap without your knowing it.

He is equally persistent about food, toys, and anything else he desires. Being extremely intelligent, he is easily trained. If he wants your approval (and he does) he'll catch on quickly and be a perfect pet. You'll have to give a lot, but you'll get a lot.

The "fashionable" prize-winning look in Siamese cats today is a rather elongated body and a long, thin, wedge-shaped head with a very pointy nose. As kittens they look very skinny, but as grown cats they take on a delicate, aristocratic look which appeals to many people. Fortunately, breeders have managed not to ruin the disposition of the Siamese in achieving this look, perhaps because they have developed it more slowly than some of the other breeds. These Siamese need a little more time to adjust and may be more nervous in the beginning than the old-fashioned type of Siamese, but once they settle in, they reveal wonderful personalities.

You can also get the round-faced, bigger-boned Siamese, or the "apple heads." Many people prefer this look and don't care in the least for prize-winning standards. These cats usually won't have papers; no breeder will bother to take them to shows as they could not possibly win anything. Their day will come again, however. Fashions change in the world of cat fancy as quickly as they do in the world of clothing. The only constant is that all Siamese have blue eyes.

People describe a Siamese by the color of his points. The points are the nose, the ears, the end of the tail, and the feet of the cat. The rest of the body is white during kittenhood, and becomes darker as the cat gets older, but there is always a very marked contrast between the body and the points.

Siamese come in Seal Point, Chocolate Point, Blue Point, Lilac Point, Red Point, and Frost Point. Seal Point is the darkest, and the color people usually associate with the Siamese. Chocolate Point is almost as dark but the points have a different, more chocolate-colored tone, and the points contrast more with the rest of the body, especially as the cat gets older. In a Blue Point, the nose is blue (or gray, depending on your own perception). A Lilac Point is a much lighter blue than a Blue. In Red Points, the color is actually closer to apricot. Frost Points are the lightest of all, some of them having almost no distinguishable points whatsoever.

Many people believe that as the color of the cat gets lighter—from Seal as the darkest to Frost as the lightest— the personality of the cat becomes less rambunctious: more rarefied, refined, and aristocratic. This is only a generalization, however, and like all generalizations, often simply not true. I have seen shy, delicate Seals and very rowdy Lilac Points. Always choose on the basis of the particular cat and by the look that happens to appeal to you, and disregard this theory.

There are also the Lynx Point and the Tortic Point. The points of the Lynx are striped instead of solid, and those of the Tortie are somewhat mottled, sometimes just an outline, sometimes with subtly graduated shadings. So far, these are only seen in the darker colors.

Burmese

The Burmese are known as the dogs of the cat family; they are dependent in the way that dogs are. A Burm can never have too much love. He will not be as insistently demonstrative as the Siamese, but somehow he'll always be near you. Often he'll simply sit and gaze adoringly at you. The Burm tends to be a one-person cat. He loves everyone, but he usually loves one special person best. When you have a party, your Burm will visit each guest in turn, jump on his lap and purr, but will eventually settle down with his favorite—his god.

I consider the Burm to be the most loyal of the bred cats, although all bred cats are extremely loyal to their favorite people. I often have a Burmese as a houseguest— her owner goes out of town— and she always has a wonderful time at my house. Maedi will not, however, give me the time of day. I'm not her adored mistress, and she'd never accept me as such—her loyalty is undying. She'll flirt with any man who comes into the house—she probably figures that's not disloyal—but never with another woman!

Typically, the Burmese is sable brown with gold eyes. There are also color variations such as Champagne Burmese and Blue Burmese, but sable brown is the classic.

Tonkinese

This breed is a cross between the Burmese and the Siamese and seems to have the best qualities of both plus a humorous slant on life that is enchanting. My cat Barny is convinced that he is Noel Coward. When he plays a joke on me, such as running out the door when I am carrying a load of laundry and can't stop him, he makes a noise like a baaing sheep—his version of a laugh.

Since this cat is bred by mating a Burmese with a Siamese, rather than by mating a Tonkinese with a Tonkinese, we do not sell these as pedigreed even though both parents are pedigreed. I understand, however, that some associations do accept them as a pure breed. To me, the pedigree makes no difference either way.

As a kitten, the Tonkinese is a medium tan color with dark points. As he gets older, he turns a deep shade of molasses but the dark points are still distinct. The eyes are either gold or blue, depending on which side of the family the cat takes after.

Abyssinian

Mr. Greer, the founder of Fabulous Felines, used to say that the Aby was a status symbol for people who hated status symbols. At first glance you may not notice his uniqueness. But look again and you will see that he resembles a wild jungle cat and is amazingly beautiful. His fur is tawny, each hair being part white, part orange, and part black. The ruddy color is very like that of lions and tigers. Some people think it resembles the wild-fur look of a rabbit. The eyes are gold and the ears alert and perky, often with wonderful little tufts of hair growing out of the ends.

These cats adapt easily and make themselves happy anywhere. They are extremely active, especially as kittens. Alert and poised to take off like a shot, they can practically fly! They are all instinct, purring happily in your lap one minute and suddenly leaping after an interesting sight or sound. They also like water and will jump into the tub with you if you're not careful, another unusual characteristic. Aby owners swear by their charm, beauty, and temperament, which combines great sweetness with great alertness.

Russian Blue

This is another wonderful cat. Russian Blue is dark gray (gray is blue in cat parlance). Some of them look just like the gray Domestic Shorthairs which are sometimes called "Maltese." The more highly bred Russian Blues, however, have emerald green eyes and an almost Slavic aspect to the face—the cheekbones are very high and the nose is long and flat. It's an unmistakable look. The tip of the fur has a silvery tinge.

These cats are the intellectuals of the cat family. In cages, they might remind you of wise little old men; they don't sell themselves at all, they just calmly return your gaze. But get one home and you will be fascinated watching him solve problems and even invent problems to solve. Once I brought home a Russian Blue kitten, because he had a calcium deficiency and needed more exercise than was possible in a cage. After his legs were back to normal (about three days), he cantered wildly around the apartment, then jumped into my lap and purred for a while, then started thinking.

On my table was a mason jar with a few crackers inside. This cat, without even one false try, figured out that he had to push the cracker to the side of the jar, then slide it up along the side to get it. It turned out he didn't want the cracker, but he pulled six more out the same way just because he was so pleased that he'd gotten it right. He also figured out, without any false tries, that to get a rolled-up cigarette pack jammed under an open door, he could first push from one side and then run around to the other to retrieve it.

This intelligence makes the Russian Blue extremely easy to train. He gets the idea immediately and will rarely need to be told twice. He's much more active than you would suppose from his tranquil manner in his cage. In fact, he's extremely active as a kitten, but he's absolutely aware of the rules of the house and enjoys pleasing you as much as he does being clever.

Other Blue Cats

The British Blue is blue all over but with gold eyes and a stocky body unlike the delicate body of the Russian Blue. He is friendly and delightful, well-balanced and usually quite calm and cheerful after kittenhood (all kittens being, of course, rambunctious).

The Chartreux is basically the same but with a slightly

grayer hue. The Korat is an excellent family pet, and noted for its intelligence.

Scottish Fold

This cat is so named because of his folded ears. They give the Scottish Fold a very cute look, almost like a little pug dog. The ear fold was a spontaneous mutation* and was first discovered in Scotland, although the cat is now bred all over. Scottish Folds come in all colors and markings, have stocky bodies, and are often polydactyl (having extra toes). Although this may not necessarily pose a problem for other polydactyl cats, the bones inside the foot of the fold are often misshapen, which may cause pain and require an operation. In some cases, the very appealing look of this cat has been bred in too fast; consult your vet about the possible need for an operation.

Rex

The Rex is another result of spontaneous mutation. The outstanding physical feature of the Rex is his sparse, curly coat, almost like a Persian lamb but not as dense and kinky. This cat lacks the outer coat of hair completely, and has only the curly undercoat. The Rex gene also contributes an unusual body type. In the Cornish Rex, the body is extremely lean and delicate, the face a fairly long wedge, and the stomach usually has a tucked-in look, almost like a whippet. In the Devon Rex, the body is stocky and the head round. Both types come in all colors and markings, and usually have amber or gold eyes.

---

*Every now and then a kitten is born with an unusual or hitherto unknown physical characteristic. When the owner of the cat finds this characteristic interesting or attractive, as in the case of the Scottish Fold or of the Rex, the kitten is bred to the parent of the opposite sex with the hope of getting more kittens with this same mutation. After this, relatives are mated for enough generations to insure that they breed the characteristic consistently.

Many people think that because the coat is sparse, the Rex will be less likely to provoke an allergy than other cats. Unfortunately, this is not true, since people are allergic to dander and/or saliva, not hair. You could just as easily be allergic to a Rex and not to a Persian.

Rexes at their best are almost overly affectionate. At their worst, because of overbreeding, they can be quirky, especially with other animals. With a Rex, I would tend to look for a pedigree that didn't bristle with too many champions—in other words, for a slower development of the strain without too many ancestors dragged to cat shows and then bred, bred, bred quickly to achieve a faddish new look.

Manx

The outstanding characteristic of the Manx is his taillessness. Sometimes he is totally tailless and sometimes he has a slight stump. His hind legs tend to be somewhat longer than average to make up for the balancing effect of the tail. The Manx comes in all colors and markings. He is steady and intelligent, neither difficult nor temperamental.

Exotics

There are many other breeds of shorthairs, many of them quite new in this country, with new breeds coming into existence all the time. The exotic shorthair, for instance, is not only a wonderful cat but a financial bargain. They resemble domestic shorthairs in that they come in all colors and markings and of course have short hair, but these cats have a bred-in disposition. Some have a stocky look unlike most domestic shorthairs, somewhat like a short-haired Persian. Others are bred with a delicate, pulled-out bone structure. The popularity of these cats increases all the time, and with good reason. They combine a good old "ordinary" cat look with the sweet, loving disposition of the bred cats—for many people the best of both worlds.

LONG-HAIRED CATS

Many people think the word "angora" describes a particular breed. The word, in fact, is a synonym for "long-haired," and is descriptive of any long-haired cat (or, indeed, other long-haired animals such as angora mice and angora rabbits). The breeds of angora cat are Persian, Himalayan, and Maine Coon.

The Turkish Angora is a long-haired white cat with a bushy tail curved in the shape of a question mark. Since this cat is called a Turkish Angora and not just an "angora," the word describes fur quality rather than a specific breed.

Persian

The Persian is a great favorite the world over because of his beautiful, long, furry hair. Usually not as bright as the shorthairs, he is calm and sweet, very loving, and placid after he passes kittenhood. He requires consistent grooming but if you make a habit of taking a few minutes every day to groom the cat, he won't develop difficult snarls. It's advisable to keep the hair clipped around the anus for the sake of cleanliness—one spot of diarrhea and a Persian can't help but become dirty.

Persians come in all colors and markings, with a stocky body and a pushed-in face. Because of the latter, their tear ducts and larynxes are often poorly developed and kittens may have a slight wheeze and teary eyes. Neither of these conditions is at all worrisome, and they usually disappear as the cat grows older.

Himalayan

The Himalayan is a cross between the Siamese and the Persian. Like the Persian, the hair is long and fluffy, but the markings are pure Siamese—Seal Point, Blue Point, Red Point, and so on—and always the eyes are blue. Though they were originally bred by mating Persian to Siamese, they now are being bred Himalayan to Himalayan, thus making them acceptable as a breed even to purists.

The disposition combines the best aspects of the two breeds. Being part Siamese, the Himalayan tends to be a bit brighter than the Persian, and being part Persian, more docile and less keyed-up than the Siamese.

Balinese

The Balinese is simply a long-haired Siamese and therefore has the same characteristics and temperament. The hair is straight, long, and silky, not puffy like the Himalayan and Persian.

Maine Coon

My own personal favorite among the longhairs is the Maine Coon. He has a very friendly, sound temperament. He also has an almost therapeutic calming effect on other cats, particularly neurotic ones. The Maine Coon often gets quite large—weighing as much as twenty to thirty pounds —and when thirty pounds of cat lie all over you, exuding goodwill, you really get the message!

The name "Maine Coon" derives from the fact that the original ones were very large and marked like a raccoon.

People thought that the Persian cats brought over by English settlers had gotten out and mated with raccoons (which is genetically impossible).

The Maine Coon now comes in all colors and markings. The fur is long, but silkier and more easily groomed than the Persian's. The body type is long instead of stocky, and the nose is long, unlike the pushed-in Persian nose. These cats often have six or more toes.

the end

INDEX

About the Author

ROZ RIDDLE shares her New York apartment with three cats. She is co-owner of Fabulous Felines, a Manhattan shop devoted exclusively to cats.